D1440714

THE AESTHETICS OF
GYÖRGY LUKÁCS

THE AESTHETICS OF
György Lukács

BY BÉLA KIRÁLYFALVI

PRINCETON UNIVERSITY PRESS

Copyright © 1975 by Princeton University Press
Published by Princeton University Press, Princeton and London

All Rights Reserved

Library of Congress Cataloging in Publication data will
be found on the last printed page of this book

Publication of this book has been aided by
The Andrew W. Mellon Foundation

This book has been composed in Linotype Electra

Printed in the United States of America
by Princeton University Press, Princeton, New Jersey

TO MARTHENA

PREFACE

Gyӧrgy Lukács was one of the leading Marxist philosophers and one of the most influential literary theorists of the twentieth century. The significance of his writings is recognized by translations in increasing numbers, not only into the languages of socialist countries, but also into French, Italian, Japanese, English, Spanish, Dutch, and others. People of letters who have found Lukács' contribution important include Alfred Kazin, George Steiner, Jean-Paul Sartre, Karl Mannheim, Susan Sontag, and Thomas Mann. To date, the translations of Lukács into English number nine volumes, but the list does not include his most significant works in aesthetics: *Specialty, as a Category of Aesthetics* and *The Peculiarity of Aesthetics*. Works about Lukács in English are few in number, with only two of the books—a collection of essays by several authors (*Georg Lukács, The Man, His Work and His Ideas*, edited by G.H.R. Parkinson) and a study only partly about Lukács (*Marxism and Form* by Fredric Jameson)—dealing primarily with Lukács' aesthetic theories. The reviews and articles that have appeared in such periodicals as the *Soviet Survey*, *Encounter*, *The Kenyon Review*, *The Journal of Philosophy*, *Marxism Today* and the *Yale Review*, while varied in subject, are brief and limited in scope. There is, therefore, a pressing need for a systematic examination of Lukács' aesthetics. The purpose of this study is to help satisfy that need.

This book is limited to an examination and exposition of Lukács' aesthetic theories. It is not a critical work, but a systematic analysis of Lukács' entire aesthetic system, intended primarily to make this important Marxist theorist accessible to English-speaking readers, since most of his works are available only in German or in Hungarian. Owing to his overwhelming familiarity with the art of literature, as compared with the other arts, Lukács draws materials for illustration and critical analysis mostly from works of literature, especially from novels and dramas. This study faithfully reflects Lukács' uneven emphasis. Further, because of my own background and interest, I have attempted to make this analysis of his aesthetic theories particularly relevant to the art of dramatic literature. This I have done by using examples taken from dramatic works, whenever it was possible without damaging the wholeness and clarity of the ideas under discussion, and by including a chapter devoted exclusively to the dramatic theories of Lukács.

Though he had been an active and prolific literary critic for more than two decades, Lukács, by his own admission, did not become a Marxist critic until the early 1930's. His early theories are built upon considerably different philosophical foundations from his late theories. Once he committed himself fully to Marxism, he rejected many of the ideas expressed in his early works. This book is limited to an examination of his Marxist aesthetic theories, for they make a coherent, whole system. Therefore, while the introductory chapter outlines Lukács' philosophical development through his entire life, the chapter on his philosophical views, intended to show the bases of his Marxist aesthetic theories, includes only the philosophical positions he held as a Marxist.

In preparing this study I read nearly all of Lukács' works (thirty-one volumes and twelve separately published essays, speeches, and interviews) either in Hungarian or in English. Where English translations were available I cited those; otherwise I translated from the Hungarian. Since most of Lukács' works were originally written in German I was conscious of the possibility of flaws arising out of double translations. To prevent any serious deficiencies I worked occasionally with German texts and, in several instances, compared my translations from the Hungarian with identical passages translated by others directly from the original German into English. To make the bibliography most useful, I have included the original German titles of Lukács' works first published in German as well as the English translation of titles not yet available in English.

A revised version of Chapter VIII was published in the December 1974 issue of *The Educational Theatre Journal*.

I wish to express my gratitude to Professor William Kuhlke and my brother László for their generous and invaluable assistance.

B.K.

TABLE OF CONTENTS

THE AESTHETICS OF
GYÖRGY LUKÁCS

1.

INTRODUCTION

T HE active writing career of György Lukács (1885-1971) spans the first seven decades of the twentieth century. An unusually prolific writer (his published works total nearly forty volumes), at the time of his death he was still engaged in writing a "truly definitive" philosophical work on Marxist ontology.[1] He was eighty-six. The changes in convictions, the revisions and rejections of earlier works, and the frequent self-criticisms that punctuate his long career are attributed by him to the necessary ideological development of a non-static thinker guided by the dialectical method and the "objective march of history."[2] Inseparable from his striving for ideological maturity was his objective to interpret Marx correctly and to show that Marxism is a unified and consistent doctrine as well as an effective and viable method in the field of aesthetic theory. Lukács does not claim to have fully understood Marx until 1931 and his definitive work in aesthetics was not completed until 1963. The theoretical works written during these thirty years (lived in difficult political circumstances) show a remarkable consistency. After the reorganizations of concepts and needed clarifications and refinements, the main ideas finally emerge logically solid and clear.

Influenced by the example of Lenin, Lukács never was an ivory-tower theorist; on the contrary, he always sought

[1] György Lukács, *Utam Marxhoz*, 1 (Budapest, 1971), p. 30.
[2] György Lukács, *Lenin* (Budapest, 1970), p. 8.

3

thorough involvement in the crucial events of his times. His political life was colorful, packed with accomplishments and failures as well as personal crises resulting in important moral and tactical decisions. Each of these had significant effects upon the formulation of his theories. In light of these factors, it is the purpose of this introduction to give a brief biographical sketch of Lukács' life, focusing on the most important influences, associations, and political and creative actions. My purpose is not so much to help the reader know Lukács the man— there are critical and expository biographies available for that[3]—but to outline the philosophical environment from which Lukács emerges and to begin the establishment of a frame of reference for the reader not familiar with him. For the same reason, the second part of the introduction, dealing with the significance of Lukács' works in aesthetics, is not a final evaluation, but an orientation and preview.

BIOGRAPHICAL SKETCH

Lukács was born on April 13, 1885, in Budapest into a wealthy Jewish capitalist family. His father apparently enjoyed a very high social status, but young Lukács was unable to enjoy the material and social benefits of upper-class life. In his writings he frequently mentions his early dissatisfaction with upper-class life style, and says that

[3] The following works in English contain ample biographical material: George Lichtheim, *George Lukács* (New York, 1970); G.H.R. Parkinson, ed., *Georg Lukács, The Man, His Work and His Ideas* (New York, 1970); Morris Watnick, "Georg Lukács: An Intellectual Biography," *Soviet Survey*, No. 23 (1958), 60-66; No. 24 (1958), 51-57; No. 25 (1958), 61-68; No. 27 (1959), 75-81.

even as a child he "felt strong urges of opposition toward
the whole of official Hungary."[4] He had an intense dis-
like for the exclusive high school he attended, where the
atmosphere was reactionary and unfavorable to learning.
The literature that first influenced him was mostly extra-
curricular, including the poetry of Shelley, Keats, and
Baudelaire, and the dramas of Ibsen, Hebbel, and Hauptmann. He read the *Communist Manifesto* rather superficially, but it was enough to introduce him to Marx.
Aspiring to become a creative writer, he wrote some
poetry and several critical essays (viewed disapprovingly
by his teachers) in imitation of the impressionistic writings of Alfred Kerr.[5]

Lukács' association with the Thália Theatre in 1905
brought an important turning point in his life. The
Thália was formed as a result of the influence of
Antoine's Théâtre Libre in Paris, and in one respect it
had similar objectives: to give adequate expression to the
dramas of Ibsen, Strindberg, Gorky, and others. But the
Thália was also a theatre for the people; playing at union
halls it brought theatre to the workers until the authorities in an ironic declaration branded the enterprise a fire
hazard.[6] For Lukács this short experience was a time of
learning. Functioning as assistant director and drama-
turg, he learned the relationship between drama and
stage. But, more importantly, it was here that he discovered that he had no talent for creative work in
literature.[7] This discovery, however, was coupled with a
newly aroused, fervent interest in criticism. Consequently, he began a period of serious philosophical study, be-

[4] György Lukács, *Magyar irodalom—magyar kultúra* (Budapest, 1970), p. 6.
[5] *Ibid.*, p. 7.   [6] *Ibid.*, p. 576.
[7] *Utam Marxhoz*, I, p. 9.

cause he "soon realized that without scientific (socio-historical) and philosophical bases no credible criticism can exist."[8]

During the ensuing five years Kant's philosophy influenced him most, although many of the Kantian ideas did not come to him unfiltered. Georg Simmel's sociological neo-Kantianism attracted him; in a distorted way, it took him closer to Marx. Even Marx, whom Lukács now studied relatively thoroughly for the first time, was seen by him "through the glasses of Simmel."[9] Wilhelm Dilthey and Max Weber, whose sociological approach to literature was vaguely related to Marx, also influenced him at this time. Lukács' works written during this period reflect this diversity of influences. *The Soul and the Forms* (1910), a work in dramatic theory that gives the first sign of his serious inclination toward philosophy, shows the influence of Simmel and Kant, while *The Metaphysics of Tragedy*, written in 1911 after he read Hegel's *Phenomenology of the Mind*, includes a strong flavor of Hegel. A more important influential factor of this period was the poetry of Béla Balázs and Endre Ady.[10] His acquaintance with Ady's poetry gave his anti-capitalistic feelings a lasting spiritual core, implanting in him a revolutionary bent that only Marx could match much later.[11] Not even Hegel, whose dialectic later brought Lukács a long way from Kant toward Marx, could match it. After all, as Lukács liked to point out, one of the basic tenets of Hegel's philosophy is "Versöhnung mit der Wirklichkeit."[12] Ady would not compromise. His poetry is an expression of the stubborn, pain-

---

[8] *Magyar irodalom—magyar kultúra*, p. 13.
[9] *Utam Marxhoz*, I, p. 10.
[10] *Magyar irodalom—magyar kultúra*, p. 8.
[11] *Ibid.*   [12] "Make peace with reality."

fully logical persistence of a human being. His questions come from the depth of human conscience; there can be no compromise in the answers.

The second decade of the twentieth century, up to 1918, when Lukács joined the Communist Party, was a period of intense "inner conflicts of contradictory world views" for him.[13] Through his writings in these years he attempted a scientific understanding of the main lines of social development as well as the philosophical problems of literature.[14] His two-volume work, *The History of the Development of Modern Drama* (1911), is such an attempt, and *The Theory of the Novel*, written in 1914-1915, shows the rejection of the neo-Kantian subjective idealism in favor of Hegel's objective idealism and, in particular, the influence of the *Phenomenology of the Mind*. Lukács wrote essays for two Hungarian periodicals, *West* and *Twentieth Century*, a collection of which were published as *Esztétikai Kultúra* in 1913. Despite his association with the two leading Hungarian literary journals, he felt an outsider among Hungarian intellectuals and artists, with the exception of his affinity for Ady and his friendship with Balázs. The feeling of ostracism, coupled with his "romantic revolutionary" attitude, colored most of his work during these years. He later considered all of his pre-World War I literary criticism defensive, a protest against the distorting and destructive effects of the life style into which he was born and from which he felt alienated.[15] This is the source of Lukács' affinity at this time with Ibsen and Thomas Mann, who were engaged in similar rebellion against their own bourgeois environments.

[13] *Utam Marxhoz*, I, p. 18.
[14] *Magyar irodalom—magyar kultúra*, p. 10.
[15] *Ibid.*, p. 14.

Between 1918 and 1930 Lukács was more actively involved in politics than in any other period of his life. In 1918-1919, after reading some of Rosa Luxemburg's writings and Lenin's *State and Revolution*, he wrote an important work in political theory, *Tactics and Ethics*, and joined the Hungarian Communist Party. He now knew where he belonged, finding his friends among the communists, whom he judged most capable of carrying through a true cultural revolution. During the existence of the Hungarian Soviet Republic, which after a few months of rather remarkable independent reign was finally crushed in August 1919, Lukács served in the government as Minister of Education and Culture. His many activities in this post have been described by one of his biographers as extremely naive,[16] and Lukács himself admitted that several of his government's policies (not excluding his own) were erroneous, mainly because the leaders were ideologically unprepared and did not understand the Marxist-Leninist method.[17] Although the reign of brutal terror that followed the fall of the Hungarian Soviet Republic was particularly vicious toward Jews and communists, Lukács stayed in Hungary for several weeks to help organize illegal underground work, going in September to Vienna, where he became chief editor (1920-1921) of the leftist publication, *Kommunismus*. Vienna at this time was a hub of exiled but active communist leaders from various European countries. Lukács was one of the most energetic men among them, writing his controversial book, *Geschichte und Klassenbewusstsein* (1923), and being involved in a number of debates over

[16] Victor Zitta, *Georg Lukács' Marxism: Alienation, Dialectics, Revolution: A Study in Utopia and Ideology* (The Hague, 1961), pp. 95-98.
[17] *Magyar irodalom—magyar kultúra*, p. 15.

tactical and theoretical issues. *Geschichte und Klassenbewusstsein*, by Lukács' own admission, was an expression of "messianic sectarianism,"[18] an idealistic doctrine asserting the imminence of socialism as a result of a gradual but inevitable historical change from capitalism. His later works, however, are enriched by conclusions derived from his practical experiences during the events of 1919, a deeper understanding of Marx, and a newly gained familiarity with some of Lenin's writings. By the end of the 1920's his Marxism was stronger than his idealism. The "Blum theses" (1929), labeled after Lukács' pseudonym at the time, reflected much more political realism and maturity, stating in essence that "the Party cannot have two strategies, republic when in legality, proletarian dictatorship in illegality."[19] The controversy over this work ended Lukács' political career, but he never ceased to consider it an important step in the development of his ability to derive theory "from the correct observation of direct reality."[20]

In 1930 Lukács went to Moscow, where he studied at the Marx-Engels Institute and began a period of working partnership with Mikhail Lifshitz. The two agreed that there was a need for a unified Marxist aesthetic as an organic part of the Marxist system.[21] In Moscow Lukács studied the newly published philosophical works of Lenin and the young Marx, among them Marx's *Economic-Philosophical Manuscripts* in which, in addition to a complete critique of Hegel, Marx clarified such questions as man's alienation in capitalism and the stages of communism resulting in humanism. Lukács began a massive reformulation of his Marxist philosophical foun-

[18] *Ibid.*, p. 17.   [19] *Ibid.*   [20] *Ibid.*, p. 18.
[21] György Lukács, *Művészet és társadalom* (Budapest, 1968), p. 8.

dations, rejecting, among other works, his *Geschichte und Klassenbewusstsein*, or, at least, admitting its methodological flaws.[22] In 1931 he went to Berlin, but after Hitler's coming to power he returned to Moscow and decided to change the focus of his work from political theory to literary theory and criticism. He started the building of "the theoretical foundations of socialist realism" in constant but disguised opposition to Stalin's cultural policies.[23]

The decade of the 1930's in the Soviet Union was a difficult one for most intellectuals. Lukács recognized that literary activity during this time required some tactical adjustments because of the dangerous political climate due to the Stalinist purges. Commenting on this in 1967 he wrote: "I believe that I wrote nothing during this period without inserting a few Stalin-quotes. Of course, today's unprejudiced reader perceives what the censor then did not notice, that these quotes have very little to do with the real, essential contents of these articles."[24] As a result of the adjustments, Lukács escaped the purges, though he was many times in the center of controversy. By 1940, however, when the magazine he worked for was officially closed, he had been stopped from publishing in the Soviet Union. Nevertheless, prior to this date he wrote or published several significant essays on the essence of realism. *The Historical Novel* (written in 1936-1937) stands out as the major achievement of the period.

In 1945, after twenty-six years of political exile, Lukács finally returned to Hungary to enjoy three years of free intellectual activity. He held an important position in

[22] *Utam Marxhoz*, I, p. 24.
[23] *Magyar irodalom—magyar kultúra*, p. 18.
[24] *Művészet és társadalom*, p. 10.

the governing body of the Hungarian Academy and was appointed professor of aesthetics at the University of Budapest. He delivered many lectures on cultural-political subjects, some of them popularized versions of his more fully developed theories. A major work in philosophy, *The Destruction of Reason,* was written during these years, though its publication was delayed until 1953. He once again flirted with political activity, but in 1948 an overt attack upon his views by the party's chief cultural spokesman, József Révai, prepared the way for his complete withdrawal. The "self-criticism" that followed the Révai debate was purely a matter of formality,[25] but the decision that he would "strive to serve the cause of communism exclusively as a theorist," speaking only for himself, was made by him in earnest and with some inner satisfaction.[26] Now he had time to begin a systematic composition of his aesthetic views.

Lukács' more or less voluntary withdrawal from active public life remained in effect from 1948 to 1956, during which time he started work on *The Peculiarity of Aesthetics* and published *Specialty, as a Category of Aesthetics.* The events of 1956, however, brought him back into political activity once more, first by expressing his opposition to the Stalinist Rákosi regime, then by participating in the ephemeral revolutionary government of Imre Nagy. After the revolt had been crushed, Lukács was deported to Romania. He returned to Hungary in April 1957, only to be expelled from the Communist Party. Party intellectuals continued to attack him sporadically until 1967, when he was readmitted to membership in the party, to enjoy grace until his death in 1971. Evidence indicates that no work by Lukács was published in

[25] *Ibid.,* p. 12.
[26] *Magyar irodalom—magyar kultúra,* p. 19.

Hungary during 1957-1967, but there was a flood of publications in 1969 and 1970.

It was during the years following his expulsion from the party that Lukács completed and published his major two-volume work in art theory, *The Peculiarity of Aesthetics* (1963).[27] Having done this, he put aside further work in aesthetics and concentrated on working out ontological problems in order to create the Marxist foundation for his proposed work in ethics. About this he wrote in 1969: "However paradoxical it may sound today, well past the age of eighty, the writing of my truly definitive works is still ahead of me."[28] Death, two years later, prevented the completion of these works, but an essay published in 1969, "The Ontological Bases of Human Thinking," gives at least a sketchy picture of the proposed ontology. True to the essence of a materialist and dialectic thinker, Lukács carried on a re-examination of theories throughout his life, bringing to them the riches of new discoveries from practical reality. At the end of his life he was convinced that after the failure of two opposing ideologies—the Stalinist dogma and the American way of life, both of which esteemed themselves as final solutions—Marxism, which had been considered obsolete for decades in the bourgeois world and which "Stalin's teachings declared official while in reality withdrew from use," had once again become timely and relevant.[29]

The Significance of Lukács' Work in Aesthetics

A study of the development of Marxist art theory and literary criticism, *Marx, Engels, and the Poets* (1967),

[27] First published in Germany.
[28] *Utam Marxhoz*, I, p. 30.   [29] *Ibid.*, p. 31.

by Peter Demetz, concludes that it is Lukács "with whom a systematic development of Marxist aesthetics commences."[30] Before Lukács' mature Marxist works, however, several significant writers worked with Marxist literary theory. Around the turn of the century two contemporaries, the German Franz Mehring and the Russian G. V. Plekhanov, were the most influential. Lukács read the works of both, at times criticized them extensively, and occasionally praised their accomplishments. But in the final analysis, he considered the theories of both inadequate and erroneous because neither "considered aesthetics an organic part of the Marxist system,"[31] and because Mehring was unable to separate himself from the "subjective idealist tendencies" of the theories of Kant and Schiller,[32] while Plekhanov, due to his extreme sociological bent, was largely responsible for the emergence of "vulgar Marxism," which contended that "art is merely an expression of a certain standpoint taken in the class-struggle."[33] A British Marxist, Christopher Caudwell, made important contributions to Marxist theory, particularly with his *Illusion and Reality* (1937), a somewhat mystical work on the magic and the collective in lyric poetry. Caudwell's mysticism and irrational tendency were rejected by Lukács.[34] Walter Benjamin, a German Marxist, who early in his life was influenced by Lukács, later became a significant contributor to Marxist theory. Lukács quoted him extensively in some of his works, acknowledging his indebtedness particularly to Benjamin's studies of baroque art, which served as a

[30] Peter Demetz, *Marx, Engels, and the Poets* (Chicago, 1967), p. 229.
[31] *Művészet és társadalom*, p. 8.
[32] *Ibid.*, p. 89.   [33] *Ibid.*, p. 322.
[34] György Lukács, *Az esztétikum sajátossága*, I (Budapest, 1969), p. 243.

13

major source for Lukács' theory of allegory in modern literature.[35] The major work of Theodor Adorno *Noten zur Literatur* (1962-1965) was published after Lukács' *Aesthetic*; nevertheless, Adorno influenced Lukács through earlier works. Having some difficulty in applying the reflection theory to music, Lukács drew upon Adorno in developing the concept of "double mimesis." The American Edmund Wilson produced his best work in practical criticism mostly in the 1930's and 1940's. He did not attempt to build a coherent, whole system of Marxist theory, trying only "to weave Marxist motifs more closely into psychoanalytic theories."[36] There is no accessible evidence showing that Lukács was even familiar with Wilson's work. The Russian scholar Mikhail Lifshitz, on the other hand, was apparently a close friend of Lukács. The chief contribution of Lifshitz proved to be *The Philosophy of Art of Karl Marx*,[37] a book in which all the remarks of Marx and Engels relevant to art are collected, arranged, and interpreted by the author.

None of the best Marxist theorists worked with the assumption that Demetz attributes to "orthodox functionaries," including Lukács, "that the utterances of Marx and Engels on literature form a carefully thought-out whole that can easily stand comparison with Hegel's aesthetics."[38] It is true that since 1932, when he made his first contribution to Marxist aesthetics in an article commenting on the Sickingen debate, Lukács defended the thesis that "Marxism has an independent aesthetic."[39]

[35] *Az esztétikum sajátossága*, ii, p. 708.

[36] Demetz, p. 231.

[37] Mikhail Lifshitz, *The Philosophy of Art of Karl Marx* (New York, 1938). This American edition is an abridged version of the original work.

[38] Demetz, p. 232.   [39] *Az esztétikum sajátossága*, i, p. 12.

14

But careful examination of his writings shows that while he considered the central task of his life to apply the Marxist-Leninist world view to areas known to him, he also set before himself the objective of developing, enriching, and elaborating this world view "insofar as this proves to be important in light of newly discovered facts."[40] This attitude makes clear Lukács' openminded, undogmatic approach to Marx. Furthermore, he did not believe that the comments of Marx, Engels, and Lenin contained an explicitly expressed system of aesthetics or even a complete outline of such, nor were they merely bits and pieces. Thus, a paradoxical situation exists: there is and there is not a Marxist aesthetic, "it must be conquered, created through independent research."[41]

By using Marx's method, instead of merely interpreting Marx's direct statements, Lukács aims to demonstrate that art as well as the aesthetic branch of philosophy go through the same dialectical-historical change as everyday human thinking, science, social philosophy, and the structure of society itself, each culminating in Marxism as its most advanced form (so far as it was then foreseeable). Showing this progression, though not primarily writing a history of art, involves using the ideas of Aristotle, Epicurus, Hobbes, Spinoza, Diderot, Lessing and Goethe, for Lukács believes that they make up the natural line of development. Excluding the concepts of philosophical idealism, this line of philosophy leads, through a dialectical evolution, to a Marxism that is a "flexible and adaptable acceptance and analysis of historical development,"[42] a Marxism that thoroughly and ration-

---

[40] *Utam Marxhoz*, II, p. 303.
[41] *Az esztétikum sajátossága*, I, p. 13.
[42] Georg Lukács, *Studies in European Realism* (New York, 1964), p. 4.

ally "searches for the material roots of each phenomenon, regards them in their historical connections and movement, ascertains the laws of such movement and demonstrates their development from root to flower, and in so doing, lifts every phenomenon out of a merely emotional, irrational, mystic fog and brings it to the bright light of understanding."[43]

The mistakes of the Stalinist era included the complete separation of Marxist thought from all previous philosophies. Lukács tries to find the continuity from Aristotle through Hegel to Marx, asserting that Marxism is not a categorically different philosophy. He often stressed that Marxism respects the classical heritage of mankind, citing Marx's fondness of the Greeks and Shakespeare in literature and his inheritance of Hegelian dialectics. "For the sphere of aesthetics this classical heritage consists in the great arts which depict man as a whole in the whole of society."[44] Consistently with this respect for the best heritage of mankind, Lukács incorporates much of German literary theory into his system of aesthetics, not at all sharing in the "blunt rejection of the whole of German culture"[45] especially in vogue after World War II. Many of these are modified but important bases, including Goethe's ideas on symbolism and allegory, Schiller's thoughts on form and content, and Hegel's dialectical view of history. Lukács' theory of the "homogen medium" of art is derived from Kant, and he accepts at least a fraction of Kant's theory of the element of "disinterestedness" in the aesthetic effect. He points out that a whole line of German art and theory from Goethe to Rilke is a rational humanist one, as opposed

[43] *Ibid.*, p. 1. [44] *Ibid.*, p. 5.
[45] Georg Lukács, *Goethe and His Age* (New York, 1969), p. 7.

16

to the line of irrationalism (lengthily discussed in *The Destruction of Reason*) from Schelling and Schopenhauer through Nietzsche to Chamberlain and fascism. Against all attacks and distortions he regards Goethe "next to Hegel, and parallel to him, as a great figure of the historical dialectic which was being realized at the time."[46]

But Stalinism not only rejected the classical heritage of the past, it also discontinued the Marxist-Leninist line in theory and practice by seriously deviating from it. Writing in 1938, at the height of the Stalinist purges in the Soviet Union, Lukács states his opposition to this in a scarcely disguised manner: "There is what is called 'publicistic criticism,' a 'purely' social or political attitude to literature, which judges past and present according to the superficial slogans of the day, without considering the real artistic content of the work in question, or caring whether it is a great work of art or a piece of worthless trash."[47] Since Stalin's death the situation has not changed significantly. In 1964, Alfred Kazin remarks that "one cannot discuss literary doctrine with Soviet writers without soon being made to feel that 'Marxism' in Russia is now just a cover for bureaucratic slogans."[48] Lukács concurs in this view of the situation, stressing (in 1967) that what has happened since Stalin is not yet a turn back to Marxism, that the rejection of the "personality cult" and the official unveiling of two or three faults of the Stalinist period are only token solutions of the problem.[49] In comments dated somewhat earlier, he

[46] *Ibid.*, p. 16.
[47] *Studies in European Realism*, p. 125.
[48] Alfred Kazin, "Introduction" to *Studies in European Realism*, p. vi.
[49] *Művészet és társadalom*, p. 8.

17

makes clear that the fight still to be won against Stalinism is difficult because the dogmatists stay behind bureaucratic shelters "reluctant to engage in sober argument," changing the old oppressive manner of resistance to optimistic assertions "that everything is in excellent order, that no further critique of Stalinism is needed, no return to the unpolluted sources of Marxism, no re-adjustment of the arts and sciences to present-day requirements."[50] It is a reasonably accurate description of the situation in the Soviet Union that in "socialist realism" the term "socialist" receives all the emphasis while "realism" very little. If the work is "socialist" by standards Lukács calls "publicistic" (meaning that it is consistent with the current declarations of the bureaucratic leadership) then it is a good work of art, realistic or not. Lukács, on the other hand, stresses unceasingly the term "realism" as the core of all art, whether socialist or other.

Lukács knows that the fight for realism has another front, where the battle is just as difficult as it is against Stalinism. He attacks "modernism" in art because of its "distorting" and "crippling" portrayal of the human being, showing that its roots are in philosophical irrationalism (see *Realism in Our Time*). From art for art's sake to naturalism he systematically criticizes every art which has not found "the path of true artistic submergence in reality,"[51] escaping instead into extreme subjectivism, irrelevant detail, or decorative formalism, largely ignoring the totality of man's existence. He criticizes also the "so-called 'purely aesthetical' criticism, a criticism approaching its subject from the viewpoint of 'art for art's sake'

[50] Georg Lukács, *The Meaning of Contemporary Realism* (London, 1963), p. 7.
[51] *Művészet és társadalom*, p. 10.

and apportioning praise or blame according to superficial formal characteristics."[52]

The full significance of Lukács' work in aesthetics will probably be more readily measurable several decades from now. So far he has influenced more philosophers and literary theorists than writers and other artists. While the components of his system are fully worked out, they are not easily accessible, primarily because Lukács' style is difficult to read; it is arid, thoroughly and painstakingly rational, and full of philosophical cross-references. He has also not been translated enough, although English translations have greatly increased in the past few years. It is my conviction, in direct disagreement with the spirit and argument of Victor Zitta's book about Lukács, that a major portion of the significance of Lukács' works comes from the circumstances in which he wrote them. Zitta considers Lukács a neurotic and an ordinary polemicist,[53] but the evidence shows that Lukács never compromised his rigorous search for truth (though he occasionally did not say it all), using the perpetually adverse conditions of his career as testing grounds for his theories. The uneven road in the development of his own theories is itself a proof that he understood the dialectical method, that he was honest rather than stubbornly defensive when the facts proved that some theory of his was of questionable validity. These factors are important to note before one embarks upon the task of studying his theories, because they help one to examine what there is in an unprejudiced manner, an attitude that has often been lacking in writings about Lukács.

[52] *Studies in European Realism*, p. 125.
[53] Zitta, p. 8, and p. 245.

2.

LUKÁCS' PHILOSOPHICAL WORLD VIEW

Is There a Marxist Ontology?

This is a legitimate question in view of the fact that evaluations of Marx's works frequently conclude that Marxism is a social philosophy with all but exclusive emphasis upon history and economics. Lukács recognizes that in the history of philosophy Marxism has seldom been seen as ontology.[1] From the point of view of idealistic philosophies and religions that assume the existence of a creator, the impression may well exist that Marx underestimates or subordinates the role of consciousness relative to the role of material being. But the fact is that "Marx conceived of consciousness as a late product in the development of material being,"[2] which, to a materialist philosophy of evolution, does not necessarily mean that it has an inferior ontological significance. Lukács adds that in one sense quite the contrary is true, since the fact "that consciousness reflects reality, and on that basis makes possible its modification through work, is, in terms of being, its real strength . . . not its weakness."[3] Asserting that Marxist thought has ontology, a "materialist historical ontology" worked out both in theory and

---

[1] György Lukács, *Utam Marxhoz,* ii (Budapest, 1971), p. 543.
[2] *Ibid.,* p. 544.   [3] *Ibid.*

practice, going beyond Hegelian logical-ontological ideal-ism, Lukács goes on to show its components.

In the process of working out a Marxist ontology, Lukács' first task is to examine the basic assumptions and final conclusions of the dominating major philosophical schools and to point to their shortcomings. This includes a small body of materialistic philosophy from Epicurus to Feuerbach, the many forms of subjective idealism from Plato through Berkeley to Kant, some aspects of contemporary phenomenology and existentialism, and objective idealism from Aristotle to Hegel. All of these philosophies, with the partial exception of the Hegelian, share one serious deficiency in their ontological answers: they conceive of being (material, phenomenal, nou-menal, essential, etc.), as basically static. Due primarily to his view of history and his dialectical conception of being, Hegel moves away from these, but not as radically as Marx. Nevertheless, in addition to the discoveries of "mechanistic materialism" and scientific evolutionary theories, Hegel becomes a major part of the foundation of Marxist ontology.

A basic ontological premise of idealist philosophy is the primacy of consciousness: there is no being without consciousness. In the case of subjective idealism, being is nearly always the product of individual, human con-sciousness, taking the form of perception, image, or con-cept. The various shades of subjective idealism are differ-entiated from one another in their assumptions, whether they postulate "outside the realm of consciousness, an objectively existing, though theoretically unknowable, be-ing (Kant's thing-in-itself) or consider everything going beyond the contents and forms of consciousness non-existent, while acknowledging the existence of only those

21

occurring in the consciousness."[4] The logic here is static, not allowing an independently existing world capable of movement, change, or evolution; it is a purely conceptual philosophy out of touch with practical reality. Objective idealism, on the other hand, while it also asserts the ontological primacy of some form of consciousness, does not at all take this to be human consciousness. In fact the latter, in a hierarchic order, is only a lower descendant, product or perhaps process of a higher objective consciousness (e.g., Hegel's Absolute Mind).[5] But even Hegel's philosophy—the most advanced form of objective idealism in which reality is seen as dynamic—is static as an entire system. In Hegel's dialectic the development is logical: Absolute Mind thinking of itself, or a rational order fulfilling itself. At a certain point, however, the change, the development of anything (having fulfilled itself), will stop. Lukács points out that "the Earth, according to Hegel, is completed when human history begins, its history has come to an end."[6]

Lukács' objection to this static quality in Hegel's philosophy is coupled with his skepticism about the existence of the objective consciousness since it is not to be found in natural or social reality. He believes that every school of objective idealism has been forced to invent some kind of myth in order to explain and justify the world-creating role of objective consciousness. He cites as examples of these myths the various conceptions of God, Plato's world of pure ideas, and Hegel's Absolute Spirit, the last of which "unifies, in a great developmental process, the whole of nature and society and man's entire material and spiritual world."[7] The source of the

[4] György Lukács, *Lenin* (Budapest, 1970), p. 165.
[5] *Ibid.*, p. 166.   [6] *Utam Marxhoz*, ii, p. 26.
[7] *Lenin*, p. 166.

skepticism is Lukács' materialism and his consequent commitment to the world view of this-worldliness that has rid itself of magic (religion), transcendentalism, or any kind of dualism. But the problem is that knowing everything in this world is impossible according to the materialistic dialectic because "the static and dynamic connection of objects, their extensive and intensive infinity does not permit that any kind of knowledge in any given form be ever conceived of as absolutely conclusive."[8] The numerous dualistic, transcendental philosophies that developed because of this problem (with particular frequency from the time of the scientific discoveries of the Renaissance), by relegating the immediately unknowable into another world, offer only an evasive, false solution. The old, "mechanistic" materialism (from Democritus to Feuerbach) does not settle the battle between this-worldliness and other-worldliness satisfactorily either. Here the world is a complicated mechanical structure, which still needs a prime mover.

The problem of this-worldliness, transcendentalism, and related ontological questions, however, did not remain unchallenged. Lukács argues that with the development of natural and social sciences in the nineteenth century, idealism (both subjective and objective) had become untenable, but since the various forms of it were helping to maintain the status quo of social systems and since historical and Marxist materialism were unacceptably radical in their implications, a "third road" was sought. In an essay, "Az egzisztencializmus" (originally published in Hungarian in 1946), Lukács predicts that "in the near future, existentialism will be the reigning

[8] György Lukács, *Az esztétikum sajátossága*, 1 (Budapest, 1969), p. 22.

23

intellectual trend in today's bourgeois world."[9] Existentialism is the "third road" that supposedly overcomes the one-sidedness of both idealism and materialism. As distinguished from materialism, where being is independent of consciousness and idealism in which being depends upon it, existentialism postulates a correlation between the two: there is no being without consciousness and no consciousness without being. Lukács contends that this philosophy as professed by Husserl, Heidegger, and Sartre solves none of the problems of ontology. It reflects, however, the predominance of fetishism and the alienation of man in modern capitalistic society. Sartre's existentialism denies the existence of collective relationships in society and makes freedom completely irrational and arbitrary by denying the connection between free choice and man's past, consequently, the ontological continuity of the personality. Lukács considers Sartre's assumption that "being is without meaning, without reason, without necessity"[10] irrational, and his narrow view of the sameness of the "human condition" as an ontologically static view. True, there is no transcendental here, only one world, but it is a disintegrated, irrational one with no understanding of man's origin, history, perspective and no indication of any relationship between man and the objective world, because the world is only some kind of vaguely alien environment in which man is "condemned" to live. Lukács calls this "refuge" of the individual into his own "intimacy" a "tragicomic dead end."[11] To a Marxist, judging it from a socio-historical point of view, the existentialist starting point that man is "thrown" into the world faced with "nothing" is "necessarily only a

[9] *Utam Marxhoz*, II, p. 98.   [10] *Ibid.*, p. 116.
[11] *Ibid.*, p. 110.

24

complementary opposite pole of that philosophical development which leads from Berkeley to Mach,"[12] that is, subjective idealism.

The Marxist materialist ontology inherits from old materialism the doctrine of the primacy of being, without underestimating the role of consciousness. Assuming a scientific-historical attitude, Marxism does not attempt to make conclusions about the origin of things any farther back than is possible to conjecture through evidence and logic. All transcendental assumptions of an original creator, prime mover, etc., are simply discarded due to their non-scientific character. What we may assume, argues Lukács, must be based on scientific evolutionary, anthropological, and historical evidence. Accordingly, we start with inorganic being producing organic being, both continuing to exist without any kind of consciousness in the universe. Then comes a significant "jump" with the development of man and the simultaneous birth of consciousness. From this moment, though a dynamic objective reality including man continues to exist independently of man's consciousness, consciousness plays an increasingly significant role in its development. Thus, man is both the product and through his essence (which is the teleological nature of his work) the producer of objective reality, particularly social reality, whose growth and contradictions within its unified development must be uncovered by the method of an historical materialist ontology.[13] On this point, the striking difference between existentialism and Marxism is that while the former, ahistorically, views only the individual man as being thrown into an alien environment, the latter, historically,

[12] *Az esztétikum sajátossága*, I, p. 23.
[13] *Utam Marxhoz*, II, p. 558.

considers man as the very product of the components of
a natural and social reality that equip him not only with
the ability to adjust to it passively (as lower beings do)
but also with the ability to alter it according to his needs.
In Lukács' ontology, as in Aristotle, man is a social
animal.

Marx took from Hegel the notion that reality is dynamic, not static. He did not see it as Absolute Mind
thinking of itself, but rather as human institutions un-
folding, changing, determined by economic forces. From
the conceptual, the emphasis is shifted to the material
bases of existence. There is no preconceived grand plan
to be fulfilled exactly; there is no end to the development;
there is only a direction that is alterable and altered by
men depending upon the degree of their awareness, including self-awareness. In Marx's materialism the starting
point is not the atom as in old materialism, nor abstract
being as such as in Hegel; in fact there is not a strict
starting point at all, because "every being must always
be an objective being, a propulsive and propulsed part of
a concrete complex."[14] This thesis, for Lukács, contains
in itself two fundamental consequences: first, that "being
is nothing else than an historical process," and, second,
"that the categories are not mere utterances about a certain being, not (idealistic) forming-principles of matter,
but propulsive and propulsed forms of matter itself."[15]

The understanding of this requires an explanation of
the Marxist view of certain key dialectical relationships
in reality. In the dialectical-contradictory unity of essence
and phenomenon, one must never be considered separately from the other. Though essence is of greater significance than phenomenon—insofar as the latter is only

[14] *Ibid.*, p. 544.   [15] *Ibid.*

an element of the former, while essence is the unified whole of those phenomena—the entire objective reality, which is a composite of all elements of phenomena, is "always richer in content than the most perfect laws"[16] derived from it. Laws (essences), however concrete, will always be only *"approximations* of the constantly changing, transforming, infinite totality of objective reality."[17] This, Lukács hurries to emphasize, does not mean relativism, because it is the essence of the dialectic method that the relative and the absolute create an inseparable unity rather than being at opposite poles. Absolute truth has its relative elements that "tie it to place, time and circumstance" while "relative truth, inasmuch as it is indeed truth, by faithfully reflecting reality, has absolute validity."[18] Of importance is that laws or essences (whether relative or absolute in the above sense) are not merely in the mind; they have a being of their own, not separately, however, from phenomena, whose independent being is also not separable from their essences.

Another dialectical relationship Lukács considers important is that of freedom and necessity. By definition man is a decision-making social animal. "Men make their own history, but not in circumstances chosen by them."[19] In society, freedom and necessity form a contradictory-inseparable unity, meaning that in man's most characteristic activity, work, teleological decisions (based on knowledge of essences), on the one hand, and their causal-compulsory preconditions (the infinite richness of reality), on the other, also form a contradictory inseparable unity. The result is that teleological plans and

[16] *Lenin*, p. 190.   [17] *Ibid.*

[18] György Lukács, *Művészet és társadalom* (Budapest, 1968), p. 263.

[19] *Utam Marxhoz*, II, p. 559.

27

means must be modified, perfected, sometimes drastically altered, because of newly discovered circumstantial environmental factors. Thus, "every progress appears as a contradictory unity of a step forward and a step back,"[20] which becomes the factor most responsible for the individual man's fatalism, pessimism, and tendency to believe in the transcendental ("Man proposes, God disposes"). Man avoids the negative effects of this problem when he fully realizes his social character: that he is not alone (again, the dialectic unity of individual and society), that he "could only change from a mere natural entity into human individuality by virtue of his social character."[21] When he also becomes aware of the dialectic unity of the external (objective reality) and the internal (man's subjective being) by means of the realization that he makes himself through his own work (the interaction of external and internal), his view of this-worldliness is complete.

Man's achievement of social consciousness and the consequent view of this-worldliness, however, does not alter the given relationship of freedom and necessity; it only opens the road to the solution of problems created by it. The above-described contradictory-inseparable unity of the two results in an uneven historical development of society. The Marxist position is that in all social development, change in the infrastructure (the economic base) is of primary importance, while the superstructure (including art, philosophy, politics, religion) is of secondary importance. Lukács argues, however, against the interpretation of those he calls "vulgar Marxists," by saying that a change in the infrastructure is not the

[20] *Ibid.*, p. 563.
[21] *Művészet és társadalom*, p. 15.

28

cause, but only a precondition for changes in the superstructure.[22] This may be taken to mean that the different areas may develop relatively independently, influencing one another, but the development of the whole is retarded (decadence sets in) if a rotten economic base does not change for a long time. In order for man to achieve the highest possible degree of freedom, the demand for it must reach down to "man's physical life, to the creation of those economic and social conditions, which institutionally secure man's complete freedom."[23]

As essential points of Marxist ontology, all of this means that change is neither predetermined nor spontaneous. There is no ultimate end, only ends that man is capable of conceiving (no further transcendence). Objective reality, its laws, and man himself are not seen as static, as unalterable. Man has the capacity to gain awareness of the dialectical laws, and the necessary freedom to guide the course and the speed of social development. The Marxist method Lukács offers is undogmatic, its chief flexibility being in the recognition of the unpredictability and "infinite richness of reality," because of which it "combines a consistent following of an unchanging direction with incessant theoretical and practical allowances for the deviousness of the path of evolution."[24]

LUKÁCS' MARXIST THEORY OF KNOWLEDGE

It is clearly evident in Lukács' writings since the 1930's that he considers philosophical idealism his arch foe. Idealism is like a many-headed monster, often appearing

[22] *Ibid.*, p. 264.   [23] *Lenin*, p. 144.
[24] Georg Lukács, *Studies in European Realism* (New York, 1964), p. 4.

29

in new shapes and disguises (existentialism, for example) seemingly impossible to destroy. Lukács believes that the major factor responsible for the persistent revival and endurance of dualistic world views, transcendentalism, and the susceptibility of human beings to their premises, lies in the nature of reality itself, that is, in the immediate unknowability of the objective world. Since rational methods do not with absolute conclusiveness answer all questions about the universe, they are mistrusted, considered inadequate, are partially or completely discarded and replaced by irrational approaches. Consequently, Lukács' endeavors to work out a Marxist rational materialist epistemology are coupled with his constant refutation of various "irrationalist" theories.

For making the original distinction between idealistic and materialistic views, Lukács' criterion is the conviction that "every epistemological question and answer depends upon how the philosopher conceives of the relationship between being and the mind."[25] Roughly, the conclusion is that in materialism being is independent of the mind but is reflected by it, while in all idealism being is a product of the mind, and that the highest, most permanent forms of being (sometimes, as in Plato, the only real forms of being) are metaphysical. To attempt to know reality, dialectical materialism considers the rational mind to be the only adequate instrument, but irrational philosophies resort to various intuitive methods, because the "reality" they wish to examine is the product of the irrational mind. The term "realities" rather than "reality" should be used here, in fact, because the major representatives of intuitive philosophies (Dilthey, Bergson, Husserl) discover drastically different "realities," contra-

[25] *Utam Marxhoz*, II, p. 83.

dictory in their structures.[26] Both the methods and the accomplishments of all irrational philosophies reveal and promote "the deprecation of rationality and intelligence, the uncritical glorification of intuition, aristocratic epistemology, the rejection of social-historical progress [and the] creation of myths."[27]

In Lukács' analysis the starting point of today's irrationalism is to be found in Schelling's aristocratic irrational view that to know the essence of reality it is necesary to possess an inborn, non-acquirable genius. This thought is further developed by Schopenhauer, while Nietzsche, advocating the domination of instincts over intellect, puts the finishing touches on the "destruction of reason."[28] Nietzsche's philosophy, in addition to being irrational, is also reactionary. Not understanding history and evolution, Nietzsche wants instead of change (the creation of something new in the world) a return to the eternal, which in Lukács' judgment is really a myth. Major non-German contributors to this originally exclusively German line of thought, such as Bergson and William James, while developing differing "realities," shared in its central premise that objective reality is not possible to know rationally and to know it can be of only technical usefulness.[29]

While the "third road"—existentialism—appears to be a departure from idealism in that it has given up the claim that anything conclusive can be said of man's real relationship with life, it remains fundamentally idealistic because it asserts "the mutual inseparability of being and consciousness."[30] Existentialism, in Lukács' view,

[26] *Ibid.*, p. 103.
[27] György Lukács, *Az ész trónfosztása* (Budapest, 1965), p. 8.
[28] *Utam Marxhoz*, II, p. 205.   [29] *Az ész trónfosztása*, p. 19.
[30] *Ibid.*, p. 320.

whether it is Heidegger's abstract duality between subjective and objective in the form of "a rigid and exclusive contrast" of the human personality and the social being, or Sartre's "being without reason," is an arbitrary, antisocial philosophy. In denying that life's perspective is theoretically knowable as a consolation to those who are not able to know the perspective of their lives, existentialism also joins in the mainstream of modern attempts to dethrone reason.[31]

Lukács never argues that any aspect of Hegel's philosophy is irrational. In fact he considers *The Phenomenology of the Mind* the direct opposite in spirit of Schlegel's irrationalism. Lukács shares Hegel's belief that every man is capable of understanding the philosophically grasped reality,[32] not meaning that common sense is enough but that through proper philosophical preparation the road is open to all. (Lenin, too, held a similar conviction.) In Hegel's world the development is logical and historical, although (idealistically) it occurs primarily in the mind and not, as in dialectical materialism, in objective reality itself only reflected by the mind. Hegel shares with all idealists (whether Plato, Schelling, or Kant) the establishment of a hierarchy in the modes of cognition, although the order is not the same among them. For example, in Schelling the artistic mode of knowledge is above all others, while Hegel puts philosophy above all. Nevertheless, in all idealism, this hierarchy is rigidly fixed, eternal, and universal.[33]

In addition to the rational approach to philosophical issues, Marx and Lukács inherit from Hegel the all-

[31] "Az egzisztencializmus," *Utam Marxhoz*, II, p. 115.

[32] G.W.F. Hegel, *The Phenomenology of the Mind*, trans. J. B. Baillie (New York, 1966), pp. 272-73.

[33] *Az esztétikum sajátossága*, I, p. 17.

important dialectical method. Since "being is a process," as we have seen Marxist ontology describe it ("the movement of contradictions," the dialectical relationship of phenomenon and essence, etc.), thinking that would adequately reproduce the original must also be dialectical.[34] The starting point of idealistic thinking, however, is contemplation in the realm of metaphysics, while in Marxism the existence of the category of metaphysics is not even recognized. Materialist dialectic is a union of practice and contemplation (excluding the metaphysical), with practice (experience) as the point of departure. Lukács repeatedly emphasizes that "in materialist dialectical theory even the most abstract categories are reflections in thought of objective reality."[35] The reversal of roles is quite evident: idealism works at the top, among the metaphysical clouds, while materialism works at the bottom, digging ever deeper for connections, laws, essences on the physical level. When Lukács says that Marx performed the operation of standing Hegelian dialectic on its feet, he means that in Marxism the dialectic derives the abstract categories from the concrete (which can only be matched, not surpassed, by abstract thought), while in Hegel the concrete has to ascend to overcome the gap and reach the abstract categories. This is not at all the same, however, as Vico's conclusion that the order of ideas must follow the order of things.[36] That would be a complete subordination of ideas, of consciousness itself, to the world of objects, which is a flaw of old materialism. Lukács believes that Marxism has been able to overcome this flaw by guiding dialectical reflection

[34] *Lenin*, p. 188.
[35] György Lukács, A *polgári filozófia válsága* (Budapest, 1947), p. 40.
[36] *Filozófiai Lexikon* (Budapest, 1953), p. 633.

33

(thinking) to set its course on the essence of reality, rather than mechanically and slavishly following every single, even accidental, movement of reality. Moreover, Marxism strives (and this may be the essential uniqueness of its dialectic) through a constant interchange of the theoretical and the practical, to approach reality's concreteness, even in its process of movement and contradictoriness, in the most perfect way possible. This gives dialectical materialism its important historical character and its consequent claim of effectiveness in dealing with totality. Lukács states that "Marxist history, as the only science, contains in itself the laws, the principles, all of philosophy's category-problems."[37] Thus, totality is seen as an historical concept (rather than the idealistic absolute metaphysical concept) based on the dialectic of the absolute and the relative. In this historical view old totalities pass away and new ones develop.

The motto of *The Peculiarity of Aesthetics* is a quotation from Marx: "Sie wissen es nicht, aber sie tun es" ("They do not know it, but they do it"). The meaning is that human beings (including idealistic philosophers in their practical lives) have always thought dialectically, but without being fully conscious of this "as Molière's Master Jourdain spoke in prose all of his life, without realizing it."[38] A fundamental thesis of dialectical materialism, that practice provides the criterion for theoretical truth, is a fact of life. The correctness or incorrectness of mental reflection of objective reality is ultimately proved only in practice. But the man of everyday life, though he can become conscious of his dialectical thinking, cannot individually utilize it to its fullest possibilities. The

[37] A polgári filozófia válsága, p. 43.
[38] Az esztétikum sajátossága, I, p. 649.

understanding of the essences (found in the phenomena) is truly adequate only if thinking is also successful in uncovering its hidden laws.[39] Reality is so complex, however, that various relatively specialized but not
mutually exclusive modes of reflection are necessary to
its understanding.

In Marxist materialistic philosophy, not only is there
no hierarchy in the modes of reflection (e.g., science,
philosophy, history, art), but all modes reflect the same
objective reality, eliminating such problems as the use of
different modes for the separate parts of a dual universe.
The case of history might serve as the best illustration of
what Lukács means by no hierarchy. He believes that the
reason Aristotle, in his *Poetics*, evaluated history as he
did, ranking it below tragedy in its effectiveness in the
quest for universal truth, was the undeveloped state of
history at the time. History was only an aesthetically
stylized recording of facts and, as such, it was mired in
particulars while appearing to work for the same goals
accomplished by tragedy. Only much later did history
develop to the point of finding its uniqueness in the
reflection and portrayal of the apparent modes, concen-
trations, and relationships of the laws of historical
development.[40] (The case of history also exemplifies
Lukács' theory of uneven development.) At the present
point of its development, history is of universal effectiveness equal to tragedy. To attempt ranking them in a
hierarchy is pointless, because the only important factor
they have in common is that they both reflect the same
objective reality. Otherwise, though they borrow tools
and means from one another, they are independent,
peculiar modes of reflection.

[39] *Lenin*, p. 189.   [40] *Az esztétikum sajátossága*, I, p. 201.

The characteristics of relative independence and peculiarity apply to all modes of reflection. Art, for example, as one kind of reflection of the outer (objective)
world in man's consciousness is a part of the general epistemology of dialectical materialism, but because of
its specialty, its peculiarity, many laws of art sharply differ from those of other modes of reflection.[41] Art is
anthropomorphic, meaning that its reflection is always
relative to man, containing man's subjective being as
well as objective reality in the form of images of the
human personality. Science, on the other hand, though
it is colored by the attitudes of individual scientists, is
disanthropomorphic; it seeks consciously to eliminate the
subjective element from the results. Lukács uses this illustration to point up the differences between the two:
"Eyeglasses do not deanthropomorphize, but binoculars
and microscopes do, because the former merely restores
the normal relationship in the whole man's everyday life,
while the latter opens up a world that would be otherwise inaccessible to man's senses."[42] Disanthropomorphic
reflection, then, while separating itself from the subjective element for technical reasons, remains a means of
man's quest to know and to dominate the objective
world. Its tools rise above the limitations of everyday
thinking, but its results are humanizing since they
broaden man's knowledge of the world. Disanthropomorphic reflection started with work, lifting "man out
of his animal being and enabling him to shape himself
into man."[43] Without abandoning his theory that both
science and art reflect the same objective reality (for man

[41] György Lukács, *Marx és Engels irodalomelmélete* (Budapest, 1949), p. 141.
[42] *Az esztétikum sajátossága*, I, pp. 165-66.
[43] *Ibid.*, p. 144.

is part of objective reality), Lukács concludes that science is *mankind's awareness* while art is *mankind's self-awareness*.[44] For art, this does not mean a "turning inside" or extreme preoccupation with the subjective being. The clarification lies in the dialectic of the objective and the subjective, for Lukács shares with Aristotle the belief that man can know himself only in and through his actions.

How important is the role of the subjective being in reflection and historical development? In Lukács' interpretation of Marxism it is of crucial importance. As we have already seen, the development of the economic infrastructure is not the cause but only an important precondition of the evolution of the superstructure. It makes changes possible, it invites development, but it does not inevitably cause it. If it caused it in the sense of natural cause and effect, then consequent changes would be predetermined and inevitable, leaving very little, if any, role for the subjective being to plan it, guide it, and influence it. Nothing illustrates the important role of the subjective being more clearly than the Marxist belief that "man creates himself," with all of his sensitivities. While not underestimating the elemental importance of the economic base (a literally starving man could not enjoy the beauty of even the most exquisite musical concert), Marx makes it unmistakably clear that only music (part of the superstructure) can develop in man the sensitivity toward music.[45] Moreover, the relationship between subject and object is reciprocal, because the musically sensitive man (subject) will in turn create and develop music

[44] György Lukács, "A művészet mint felépitmény" (a special publication of the Hungarian Cultural Ministry, 1955), p. 7.

[45] Mikhail Lifshitz, *The Philosophy of Art of Karl Marx* (New York, 1938), p. 62.

(object) and so on. In the process the human being creates, develops himself.

The dialectical relationship of subject and object invades all areas of life. The primary human activity, work, is teleological (it is planned and purposeful). In practice, human beings cannot recognize either pure subjectivity or pure objectivity.[46] On the one hand, even the most objective discovery (law, fact, etc.), is the result of a subjective effort. On the other hand, man's subjectivity, his inner world, cannot be known in its complexity and depth without a thorough understanding of its context, the objective world. There is no sense of duality here; the connection is organic and dialectical.

That leaves only the examination of the inner characteristics of the subjective being. Lukács rejects the thesis of modern philosophies that intuition is a separate, independent mode of knowledge, diametrically opposed to the rational. Nor does he accept the idea that there are ontological realms conquerable only intuitively. To him intuition is simply a part of the rational mind, "a psychological component of every scientific method of work." Psychologically, intuition means that "the unconsciously flowing thinking process suddenly becomes conscious."[47] The reverse is also true. There are many instances of unconscious behavior that had originally been conscious, but later, through habit, convention, and repetition, became instinctive, unconscious.[48] A positive example of the conscious becoming unconscious is an artist (e.g., an actor) or a scientist who functions in specific advanced areas with the most elementary principles that were some

[46] *Művészet és társadalom*, p. 14.
[47] *A polgári filozófia válsága*, p. 84.
[48] *Az esztétikum sajátossága*, I, p. 83.

time ago very much in his conscious, now only in his unconscious.

The conclusion of Lukács' argument, then, is that intuition is an organic part, a completion of the conscious, rational thought process. In light of this, he considers the theories, for example, of Freud, in terms of the conclusions they lead to in aesthetics, too eccentric, because they extend a possibly partially important factor (e.g., sexuality) into an all-moving force. Thus he recognizes essentially only conscious human behavior as significant. But, before he closes the door on this subject, he points out another factor less frequently examined by theorists. This factor is false consciousness, or the incorrect conception of plan and intention. In human work failure is the result of false consciousness, manifested only when the discrepancy between plan and result is evident. For example, atomic energy was planned to benefit man, but the result was the atomic bomb, threatening to destroy man. This problem is far more difficult than whatever problems are posed by the unconscious, because the complexity of society is filled with conflicts arising out of individual and class differences.[49] Even where such differences do not exist, the results often differ from the intentions. Lukács' answer: only the rigorous, disciplined application of materialistic-dialectical thinking can control the problem.

[49] *Utam Marxhoz*, ii, pp. 552-54.

3.

THE ORIGIN AND DEVELOPMENT OF ART

Just as it is not possible to explain the life of a tree without the consideration of its roots and the soil to which those roots are connected, so is every attempt doomed to failure that would understand a particular work of art separately from the soil of its origin. This is an essential principle of Marxist aesthetics. Lukács emphasizes repeatedly that the historical *hic et nunc* is an unavoidable and inseparable component of not only every work of art but every human action and attitude. Individual pieces of art grow out of the deepest endeavors of the age of their origin.[1] This basic assumption has several important implications for a theory of art. The most important of these, universality and individuality, will be discussed in connection with the special category of aesthetics in Chapter v. One crucially significant implication, however—that the origin and development of art is a social-historical phenomenon—should be discussed here.

In broad terms of dialectical materialism, human life consists of the individual and collective interaction of human beings (as objective and subjective beings) and

[1] György Lukács, *Az esztétikum sajátossága,* I (Budapest, 1969), p. 22. Further references to this work in this chapter will be identified parenthetically (by volume and page) in the text.

40

the objective world. Individuals die, but humanity lives on, collecting and utilizing past accomplishments and achieving constant, though uneven, progress. The earliest human activities satisfy only the most immediate needs, in terms of devising the most primitive means of adjusting to the objective world, or, in some cases, adjusting some aspects of the physical world to human needs. Every means devised is "inherited," acquired, perfected, and passed on by succeeding generations. Still, in primitive life man has very little perspective. In contrast, modern man has a relatively broad perspective of past and future life. Consequently, not all of his endeavors are directed to the satisfaction of immediate practical needs. Numerous specialized areas have developed (science, philosophy, art, religion, etc.), many of them at a considerable distance from a readily perceivable direct connection with either immediate or practical needs. Nevertheless, Lukács firmly believes that all human endeavors, primitive or modern, have one thing in common: they grow out of and feed back (directly or indirectly) into the needs of social life. In the introduction to his *Aesthetics*, he puts this concept in the form of the following metaphor: "If we imagine everyday life as a great river, then reality's receptive and reproductive forms of a higher order, science and art, branch off, become differentiated from it, and develop in accordance with their peculiar aims, achieving their pure forms in this peculiarity which was brought into existence by the needs of social life, only to join once again the river of everyday life by virtue of their influence upon the lives of men. This [the great river] then, constantly enriched by the most remarkable accomplishments of the human mind, assimilates them . . . to branch them off once more

41

as higher objective forms of new questions and demands"
(1, 9-10). This is not to be interpreted as a simple utilitarian conception of the function of art. Lukács does not
believe that art has either direct practical effect or direct
practical value for man and society. (See Chapters VIII
and x for a discussion of these.) What is important here
is Lukács' firm belief that human activity develops dialectically, progressing toward greater and greater perfec-
tion of both means and ends, toward the improvement
of the quality of human life.

Not all modern thinkers share this rather optimistic
Marxist concept of progress. Some philosophers (e.g.,
Nietzsche) believe that progress is one of many myths
fabricated by man. In view of this, the objective source
of the belief in human progress might be demanded. The
source is the Marxist view of history, which differs considerably from traditional approaches to the subject. In
the context of a dialectical materialist philosophy, Marxism opposes the viewing of history as almost exclusively
political history going back only as far as written records
allow it. Marxism considers human prehistory a continu-
ation of natural history. Its study of human prehistory
reaches back as far as ¾ million years, examining early
man's environment through geology and paleontology,
and the entire scope of cultural, economic, political, and
religious activities of primitive communities through the
discoveries of anthropology, which examines early man's
physical makeup, and archeology, which is concerned
with what man made and the changes in human culture.
In this long and broad view of the past, despite the many
diversions and retrogressions, it is possible to define progress scientifically. Judging from the vast amount of available physical evidence, cultural progress never starts from
a blank page; rather, it incorporates the achievements of

earlier ages in accordance with its present needs.[2] Progress is cumulative, the present always taking possession of the broadened awareness, self-awareness, and the best values of past generations, but it is also uneven in that some aspects of man's awareness may remain stagnant for thousands of years, while others develop at a rapid pace.

In this theory, two aspects of the development—(1) that it is cumulative and (2) that it occurs in man's consciousness—mark the qualitative difference between men and animals. Animal development is merely physiological and therefore slow, passive, and inflexible, while man's development is mental and therefore flexible, active, and cumulative, hence also progressive. Gordon Childe's statement that "progress in culture has, indeed, taken the place of further organic evolution in the human family,"[3] underscores Lukács' theory that while lower beings adjust to their environment instinctively or biologically, human beings alter the environment itself, consciously and culturally, to suit their own needs. With the mastering of fire, speech, and various tools (with work) man made himself; asserting his humanity, he became a creator.[4] To both Marx and Lukács work is the key factor; with work humanity was born. Lukács, of course, differentiates between animal, instinctive type of work (bees, spiders) and human work, which is always teleological in nature (I, 33). He also asserts that human work is always both mental and physical (not only abstract, mental work, as in Hegel), and that work and speech

[2] György Lukács, A különösség, mint esztétikai kategória (Budapest, 1957), p. 238.
[3] V. Gordon Childe, Man Makes Himself (London, 1936), p. 33.
[4] Ibid., p. 50.

originated at the same time. It follows then that Lukács considers work as the original mother of all human development, including art. He rejects, however, the idealistic "myth" that art was born with man, that poetry is the mother tongue of mankind, arguing that artistic reflection began at a fairly advanced stage of man's development, progressing very slowly and gradually until it achieved its peculiarity. The separation of art from religion started even later, advancing at a slower and more uneven pace, and it is still unfinished today.

The first stages in the long history of the development of peculiar artistic reflection consist of the development of certain preliminary abstract forms that by themselves do not constitute art, but become essential components of art at later stages. These abstract forms are rhythm, symmetry, proportion, and decorative art. Lukács rejects the idealistic theory that rhythm is a human characteristic given from above, and the Aristotelian assumption in the *Poetics* that the sense of rhythm is natural to man. To the degree that rhythm is natural, man shares it with animals, and to that same degree it is not uniquely human. Animal rhythm is spontaneous and inborn, while uniquely human rhythm is developed and perfected by man through conscious practice. The various forms of rhythm get into our consciousness as, for example, sounds that are originated when tools come into contact with materials (1, 234). Rhythm makes work more efficient and easier both physically and psychologically, and for those reasons it is cultivated with a sense of pleasure. At this point, however, rhythm is still merely a factor of everyday life; only later, through ritual dances, singing, and music, which are also directed toward practical needs, does it become a reflection of those factors of life (1, 242).

44

Proportion and symmetry, characteristics of the objective world, were also discovered by man through work. As a result he created proportionate and useful tools, while making the process itself more efficient (1, 270). Further, one may conjecture that the successfully made tool (e.g., ax or arrow), being easy to handle and very useful, caused joy in the creator, and the pleasure thus aroused already contained in it the seeds of pleasure in the aesthetic sense. Proportion, symmetry, and rhythm, already understood and mastered by man, became the bases of decorative art in the next phase of development. Man may have first decorated his tools and perhaps his body because nature had not decorated him as it had other creatures (1, 287). Decorative art aspires to aesthetic evocation, but its appeal is only formal, reflecting primarily inorganic (e.g. geometric) beauty. Its aesthetic value surpasses that of its components because it is not merely useful, but it swings in the other extreme by being almost exclusively pleasant. Objects of decorative art are contentless, worldless, always referring only to themselves (1, 311). Lukács differentiates aesthetic works from merely useful or merely pleasant creations on the basis of their ethical-human contents. The core of aesthetic beauty is to be found in this ethical content, expressed in appropriate artistic forms.

What has been discussed so far—the development of abstract forms in the human consciousness—is described by Marx as "the richness of subjective human sensibility—the ear for music, the eye for beauty of form, in short, sensibilities capable of human enjoyment, sensibilities which manifest themselves as human powers."[5] These outline the borders of the area of art, but not

[5] Mikhail Lifshitz, *The Philosophy of Art of Karl Marx* (New York, 1938), p. 62.

45

rigidly, because human sensitivity continues to develop through the ages both qualitatively and quantitatively. Potentially, these sensibilities constitute all of the basic subjective elements that later separate anthropomorphic and disanthropomorphic reflections, art and science. The first known "art" works, cave paintings discovered in France and dating back to the Aurignacian phase of the Old Stone Age approximately thirty thousand years,[6] show a blend of anthropomorphic (art, magic) and disanthropomorphic or scientific reflection. The paintings were presumably produced by hunters in dark, low caves deep underground, accessible only by crawling and visible only by the aid of artificial light. They were obviously not done for viewing pleasure, nor to satisfy sudden artistic impulses, because they are products of long periods of painfully difficult work. The paintings show two-dimensional animals with arrows and darts in them as the hunters wanted to see them in life for their economic purposes. They were intended as magic, to conjure up in the outside world what the community needed. Much pain was taken by their creators to make them realistic and accurate in detail. In this example it is impossible to separate the magical, artistic, and scientific factors. Gordon Childe believes the paintings were practical in aim and "designed to ensure a supply of those animals on which the tribe depended for its food."[7] Other "arts" of ancient men were probably done with similar aims in mind. The stone figurines of women of the Aurignacian phase with sexual features exaggerated were probably fertility charms, and the neolithic rites were performed to ensure fertility, food, hence survival.[8]

In further analysis Lukács' main objective is not to

[6] Childe, p. 61. [7] *Ibid.*, p. 62.
[8] *Ibid.*, p. 103.

pinpoint chronologically the separation of art from the apparent early mixture of reflective modes, but to explain why and how they separated and what is unique to each. It must be kept in mind that Lukács' ontology admits of one unified world only; consequently, all of the reflective modes compared here, including religion, are reflections of that one objective reality. Religion and art reflect the world anthropomorphically through the involvement of man's subjective being, while science strives to reflect it disanthropomorphically, through objective instruments. To some degree, however, both subjective and objective elements enter into the methods of each; therefore they are not totally exclusive categories.

In an attempt to explain the objective world and to adjust himself to it, early man creates gods as corporate personifications of his hopes and fears and of everything otherwise unexplainable. In short, the gods are the personifications of his ignorance. Through various rituals and magic he attempts to entreat the gods for help and favors. More often than not his efforts are "rewarded" because nature's seasonal changes occur with relative regularity. Occasional accidents and irregularities may then be taken as a direct result of improper execution of the rites. Thus he invests his faith in these rites and continues to perform them in that spirit regularly, punctually, and fervently. In the performances he further develops those subjective sensibilities (e.g., rhythm) essential in the later development of art. But this is not yet art, nor is it science, though magicians and priests masquerade as "scientists." Gordon Childe explains the difference in this way: "Man performs the magic rite because he believes in magic, not to see what will happen. His society is convinced of the efficacy of magic; testing is unthinkable. The attitude of the magician is diametrically op-

47

posed to that of the experimental scientist."[9] In Lukács' judgment, magic and religion are organic parts of man's "everyday" life, because the subjective being always enjoys primacy over any kind of objectification (I, 113). The title character in Alexander Solzhenitsyn's novel *One Day in the Life of Ivan Denisovich* may help to illustrate this. Ivan believes that the old moon breaks up into pieces every month. What happens to its pieces? Well, it is plainly visible that stars are constantly falling out of the sky, creating numerous gaps. The bits and pieces of the old broken moon serve to fill in these gaps. Ivan's explanation is obviously an old, traditional, superstitious tale. It is an example of an attempt by man to explain the objective world outside of himself anthropomorphically. But man's senses alone prove to be inadequate for the task, the resulting "solution" is full of the errors of "everyday thinking." Art, religion, and everyday thinking cannot solve such a problem; only deanthropomorphized reflection can.

Before deanthropomorphized reflection became highly developed, however, religion embraced all aspects of human endeavor. The seeds of what later developed into art, science, and philosophy were built into its system (II, 722). Theologically dogmatized faith dominated all modes of reflection and cognition. The separation of science from religion was a relatively easy process. As a result of quickly accumulating scientific achievements, and the consequent development of scientific thinking, men drew a distinction between faith in religion and faith in science. The former (e.g., faith in the resurrection of Christ) always comes from opinion, an attempt at explanation that cannot be verified, leads to a blind

[9] *Ibid.*, p. 226.

alley, and becomes faith. The latter (e.g., faith in the expertness of one's doctor) is the result of verification and can be verified again and again. Religion, unable to compete and coming into frequent conflicts with science, pulled back into a pure concern with the subjective man and the transcendental world (1, 113).

The two most pure forms of anthropomorphic reflection, religion and art, however, continued to manifest themselves in frequent, mutual entanglements. The similarities of the two are substantial, because the central subject of each is man, and the method of reflection is through man's consciousness in both. Lukács draws the differences between religion and art, starting with their respective relationships to the objective world. Religion's concern is primarily other-worldly, while art's is exclusively this-worldly. The other, transcendental, world of religion, asserted to be a truer reality than the reality of everyday life, took its origin from man's first subjective alienation from physical reality. The religious man's relationship to the gods who make up the transcendental world is that they are "fantastic reflections of his own essence, whom he created, but whom he worships as alien powers dominating him."[10] Thus, religion's connection with objective reality is very thin, because its reflection of objective reality is really a reflection of man's alienation from it through the resulting distorted emotions. In religion, then, both the central subject and the medium of reflection are only man's subjective being. Art, on the other hand, is a reflection of the whole man (subjective and objective) because it is the result of mental work, of an observation of man's deeply rooted relationship with the many facets of the physical world, in

[10] György Lukács, *Utam Marxhoz*, II (Budapest, 1971), p. 288.

49

short, of an "artistically conscious attitude" (I, 401).
Furthermore, art, in its fictional elements, consistently
admits their fictitious characteristics; it does not attempt
to lie about them. Art is understood as art by both artist
and audience, as opposed to magic, rite, and ritual, which
demand that all participation, all emotions, be real. "It is
part of the essence of aesthetics that the reflected image
of reality is conceived of as reflection, while magic and
religion attribute the status of objective reality to their
systems of reflection and require belief in them" (I, 350).
Lukács cites the theories of both Diderot and Stanislav-
sky to argue that in acting, for example, the most even,
the most consistently high-quality achievement is not the
result of spontaneous, direct emotional living-through,
but of evocation of emotion through consciously applied
technique.

As a method of reflection, art becomes independent,
gains its own identity through consciousness. Manifested
in dialectic thinking, this artistic consciousness is capable
of satisfying the demands of a changing, dialectic reality.
Lukács believes that the cause of Socrates' rejection of art
is a "defense of religious traditions against the endeavors
of art, which wants to reflect the changing reality in new
forms, in accordance with the real changes" (II, 635).
Despite the accomplishments of Aristotle in correctly
describing artistic truth, the autonomy of art, the relationship of ethics and art, and the aesthetic effect, art
was for many centuries an instrument of religion. The
intention was to teach dogma to the masses through
"theology expressed in artistic images" (II, 672). It seems
that the struggle to separate art from religion, which
started in the Renaissance, has come to a successful end
today. Lukács maintains, however, that the so-called
"avant-gardist" art of the twentieth century has brought

about a relapse, reviving a "religiously constrained art" through the domination of the allegorical style (II, 673).

Art may be transcendental, but only in the sense that its accomplishments often transcend the immediate needs of social reality. It is entirely possible that any particular artist's objective endeavors, "founded in the social-human essence of art," become effective only centuries or millenniums later. Nevertheless, in this endeavor his art remains this-worldly. To the same degree, and with similar qualifications, even science is "transcendental." While religion concentrates on the individual man's future, seeing it in the "other world" and working toward its redemption there, science and art focus their efforts on the future of mankind, seeing it in "this world" only. Thus, this-worldliness marks the link between art and science, but the differences between the two are as important as those between art and religion. Lukács points out that the "amendation of artistic truth with the help of scientific truth" has been a frequent occurrence in the history of art and art criticism (II, 630). From Plato's demand (*Ion*) for accurate, expert knowledge secured from the specialized expert himself, through Zola's attempts to apply scientific methods in his naturalistic writings, to today's "literature based on a montage of documents" (II, 630), the mixture of scientific and artistic modes of reflection has been a constant problem. Lukács puts the core of the differences in this way: "Art creates the world of men, always and exclusively. . . . In every facet of the reflection (contrary to scientific reflection) man is present as a determinant: in art the world outside of man only occurs as a mediating element of human concerns, actions and feelings."[11] The objective world (outside world) is, of course, present as the

[11] A *különösség, mint esztétikai kategória*, p. 235.

historical *hic et nunc*, because without it the reflection of man would be isolated, incomplete, but it is reflected from the point of view of man. Art, then, is both anthropomorphic and anthropocentric.

Based on the above factors, art is also necessarily committed. All works of art, even those seemingly most distant from social life, unavoidably contain in themselves the attitudes and commitments of the artists.[12] Scientific achievements (e.g., discoveries) are characterized by an inherent detachment. No individual's or community's standpoint alters the fact that the earth revolves around the sun.[13] The controversy over Copernicus' discovery was not about an objective truth, but the social consequences of that objective truth. Science approaches all of its problems with the same objectivity; it is not anthropocentric.

There is a broad borderline area between science and art and everyday life, which Lukács considers to be the cause of much confusion. Art's effect is direct and immediate only in the aesthetic sense, not in the practical (e.g., ethical) sense. The most purely scientific achievements, such as the understanding of electromagnetic principles, have no direct, immediate effect of any kind. Only long after the discovery of those principles, in the form of streetcars for example, do they have an effect on the everyday life of man. Once that happens, however, the effect of scientific achievements is concrete, perceivable, and verifiable. Not so with art, whose belated practical effects are enriching and humanizing, but only unevenly, contradictorily, and to differing degrees with individual men. Several borderline areas, however, related

[12] György Lukács, "A művészet mint felépitmény" (a special publication of the Hungarian Cultural Ministry, 1955), p. 16.
[13] *Ibid.*

to both science and art, but closest to everyday life (e.g., rhetoric, reporting, publicistic writing) do aspire to a direct practical effect and often achieve it. These borderline cases apply artistic methods, but they are not art: they do not create their "own world" as art does and do not evoke an aesthetic effect. A play, for example (such as *King Lear*), that is art does not persuade the viewer to go out and do a specific thing as rhetoric does, or correct a wrong as reporting does, nor does it attempt to dissuade him from engaging in a certain activity as a sermon does. A play's effects (as all art's) are not measurable in one audience or one generation; rather, they are accumulated in man's self-awareness, never to be erased.

It follows from this that Lukács (having discussed religion as false cognition and distorted self-awareness, consequently a negative factor) considers science to be mankind's cognition (consciousness) of the objective world and art as mankind's self-awareness (self-consciousness) and, by virtue of its cumulative effect, the memory of mankind. Art arose from the needs of everyday social life, along with religion and science, and through its development has found its unique method of changing life's problems into peculiarly aesthetic forms. Its accomplishments are the "aesthetically conquered" aspects of reality, which penetrate the fabric of everyday life unceasingly, enriching it in both the objective and the subjective sense (I, 198).

4.

THE THEORY OF AESTHETIC REFLECTION

O<small>NCE</small> Lukács began to make systematic contributions to Marxist aesthetics (from the early 1930's) the theory of aesthetic reflection gained central importance in his works. Four decades of writings contain innumerable examples, illustrations, clarifications, negative definitions, analogies, and references to previous and contemporary authorities on the subject, but never the final conclusive definition, say, in the manner of Aristotle. The reasons are simple: materialistic dialectic does not permit conclusive definitions (they are static), only flexible "determinations." The theory continued to evolve in his mind until *The Peculiarity of Aesthetics* (1963), and, while the concept of aesthetic reflection is simple at its core, its interrelatedness with other important aesthetic principles is quite complex. Because of the complexity of the issue, what follows here is somewhat crippled, though hopefully not distorted, without the benefit of the content of the subsequent three chapters. Yet, for the sake of clarity, it is necessary to start with a relatively isolated discussion of the concept, for the theory of aesthetic reflection is undoubtedly the framework and backbone of Lukács' entire aesthetic system.

In many of his discussions of artistic reflection Lukács states at the outset that the theory is not original with Marxist aesthetics. Whether it was called mimesis, imitation, or sometimes representation, it has been held important by a long line of theorists since Aristotle, and the best artists created according to its principles. On this point, as on many others' Marxist philosophy and aesthetics has a strong link with the best traditions of the past. Lukács knows that many people, including communists, are astonished to find that Marxist art theory is so deeply rooted in classical traditions: "That the Marxist aesthetic in this central question makes no claim to radical innovation is only surprising to those who without any serious reason or real knowledge of the matter link the proletarian world view to some kind of radically new, artistic 'avant-gardism,' who believe that in the realm of culture the liberation of the workers means a complete break with the past."[1] Lukács firmly believes that the new culture to be created by the liberated working classes in socialist countries will be, and can only be, based on the thousands of years of cultural accomplishments of mankind. In this heritage, reflection is of central importance. Only the representatives of "bourgeois subjectivism" and irrationalism protest passionately against it, seeing "the abasement of the 'holy' subjectivity and the 'limitless' creative ability in the tying of artistic fantasy to reality and objective necessity."[2] Lukács' answer to this protest is based upon the premises of dialectical materialism when he comments that "duly considered, all we do, all we know and all we are, in the final analysis, is the product of our reaction to reality."[3]

The term "reflection" conjures up the image of the

[1] György Lukács, *Marx és Engels irodalomelmélete* (Budapest, 1949), pp. 142-43.
[2] György Lukács, *Művészet és társadalom* (Budapest, 1968), p. 13.
[3] *Ibid.*, pp. 13-14.

mirror, hence a photographically faithful portrayal of life, even the "slice of life" theory of the late nineteenth-century naturalist trend to which most twentieth-century artists and theorists have a deep-seated aversion. It is not in the naturalistic sense that Lukács uses the term. He clearly rejects all naturalistic theories of art, primarily through the refutation of the prescriptions of Zola, and he systematically criticizes most of the works of Strindberg, Zola, and Hauptmann that show a tendency in that direction. Why, then, does he insist upon the use of the term "reflection"? He explains that the mirror image, though not to be taken literally, is necessary because only through it can a fundamental premise of art be made clear: that art reflects the reality that exists independently of our consciousness.[4] In Lukács' system the term "reflection" is a constant reminder of the objectivity of art, but it definitely does not have a passive, mechanical meaning, with implications of copying, photography, or any kind of naturalistic technique.

A brief examination of the nature of human perception, as understood by Lukács, is necessary here. The basic question is "how does the picture in the consciousness relate to objective reality?"[5] Lukács argues that man is not an objective scientific instrument or measuring device that simply records things that reach his brain by way of his various senses. Rather, man subjectively responds to each split second of sense experience, the main feature of the response being selection, or the sorting out of the essential from the non-essential. This, however, is

[4] *Ibid.*, p. 285.

[5] György Lukács, *Az esztétikum sajátossága*, 1 (Budapest, 1969), p. 326. Further references to this work in this chapter will be identified parenthetically (by volume and page) in the text.

not an arbitrary selection-response, but a selection guided by the subjective and objective components of the total situation. The subjective selects from the infinite complexity of the given phenomenon those elements which are really important to the present situation.[6] The subjectivity evident in the selection process of a real life situation is based on the vital interests basic to man's existence. But, while both the subjective and objective are at play in each case, the selection process will not be successful (in terms of man's vital interests) unless the subjective is able to select from a complex phenomenon (e.g., an approaching automobile) the objective essentials (time, speed, mass, etc.), inherent in that phenomenon. The successful selection of the subjectively essential factors depends upon man's understanding of the objectively essential factors. Hence, the correct understanding of the dialectical relationship of essence and phenomenon is fundamental to life. This conception of the nature of human perception goes beyond both empiricism and mechanistic materialism (the philosophical foundations of naturalism), which contend that only phenomenon is important, that the mind's role is merely to give names to specific phenomena, but avoids the other extreme, idealism, which attributes a metaphysical existence to essences, separated from phenomena (1, 329-30).

The above principles apply with equal force in artistic reflection. The selection of essentials means in art the portrayal of the typical, a degree of generalization, but without the creation of mere abstractions. Mankind is never shown as an independent entity, dualistically separated from its individual members; it is shown in the form of individuals and individual destinies (1, 225). Nor

[6] György Lukács, "A művészet mint felépitmény" (a special publication of the Hungarian Cultural Ministry, 1955), p. 4.

57

is the artist seen by Lukács as an independent entity doing his work guided only by his personal aims, fancies, whims, and prejudices. The artist, as the subjective element doing the selection, in addition to being an individual with his special set of sensitivities and experiences, is also a representative (one might say an agent) of mankind. This is important because in both life and art the breadth and depth of every expression and communication attempt "depends upon the breadth, greatness, and depth of that world, which, as the material of reflection, has accumulated in the subjective, and which determines the expression both directly and indirectly" (ii, 306).

The peculiarity of aesthetic reflection, in addition to its anthropocentric quality and this-worldliness, is its ability to achieve the unity of seemingly contradictory elements of reality. Lukács sees as the goal of every great art the rendering of such a picture of reality in which the contradictions of phenomenon and essence, subject and object, the particular event and the law, the direct experience and the concept, internal and external, form and content, static and dynamic, etc., are dissolved in such a way as to form a spontaneous, inseparable unity in the receiver during the direct experience of the art-work.[7] The art-work, then, is capable of surpassing reality as seen by the man of everyday life, the receiver, and can provide him with a "more faithful, fuller, livelier, more dynamic" reflection of that same reality than he otherwise possesses,[8] and can afford him a deeper, more concrete glimpse of some aspect of that reality (in which he himself lives, feels, thinks, and acts) than the bounds of his own experiences, and generalizations based upon them, would permit.

[7] *Művészet és társadalom*, p. 119.
[8] *Ibid.*, p. 120.

When we look at what Lukács' reflection theory has to say about the internal characteristics of the individual art-work, we see clearly how distant Lukács is from naturalism and how close his affinity with Aristotle. In his view even if a work of art is a composite of the most accurate, most photographically faithful details that it is humanly possible to assemble, in its wholeness it still may be the most distorted, subjective, and arbitrary reflection of reality "because a thousand accidents placed side by side never result in necessity."[9] On the other extreme, it is possible to imagine a work of art in which none of the parts (separately from the whole) bears any resemblance to any specific aspect of objective reality, yet in their wholeness make up a great work of art. It is the relationship of the totality of the art-work's "own world" to objective reality that is the crucial factor, and even that not in terms of a literal resemblance between the two but, rather, in terms of the art-work's accurate reflection of the total process of objective reality,[10] because reality (being) is not static, it is an historical process. Consequently, any particular part of an art-work, whether it comes from the artist's direct observation and experience or merely from his fantasy, can be evaluated regarding its artistic correctness or incorrectness solely on the basis of its contribution to such a total artistic reflection. The improbable, fantastic, and grotesque particulars in works, for example, by Aeschylus, Dante, Cervantes, and Goethe (all of whom Lukács considers great artists) are seen not only as acceptable but as necessary by Lukács' Marxist theory of reflection.

Action, central to Aristotle's treatment of poetry, is also a significant factor in Lukács' aesthetic reflection. He agrees with Aristotle that "life consists in action"

[9] *Ibid.*, p. 125.   [10] *Ibid.*

(*Poetics*, vi, 9) and considers action as one of the forming principles of artistic reflection. But action implies movement, time, and space, and it is in this broader sense that Lukács examines its relationship to reflection. Time and space are "man's natural environment" (1, 648). It is impossible to conceive of action without the presence of both. There is a dialectical relationship between time and space: there are such elements of reality as quasi-space and quasi-time. It is meant to be more than a metaphor when he says that "time is the space of human development" (1, 653). He recognizes that time may be isolated from space as a "thing-in-itself," but in relation to man neither can occur separately. Since art is always in relation to man (it is anthropomorphic) no aesthetic theory should isolate time and space metaphysically (as Kant and Bergson had done). In the visual arts, for example, the portrayal cannot be only of the moment; the finished work must contain in itself the factors of movement (or quasi-time), otherwise the portrayal will be only mechanically faithful. The movement should be portrayed in such a way that, without the destruction of its presentness, the art-work's "wherefrom" and "where-to" be evocatively sensuous (1, 657). That is the objective side of time in "space art." The subjective side of it is in the fact that the taking-in or viewing of works of visual art does not consist of an arrested moment, but of long and repeated examination (1, 657).

Of music, however, it is not enough to say that it contains quasi-space in the totality of its world. By its apparent high degree of abstraction, music poses more problems for Lukács' reflection theory than any other art form. Lukács is aware of the criticism directed at his theory, because many people doubt the mimetic characteristic of music and use this area to refute the general applicability of reflection (II, 306). He insists, however, that the theory of reflection applies to all art, and gives the following argument to explain its presence in music. The subject of music is "men's inner life," the reflection is of their "inner world" (II, 307). This fact does not mean pure subjectivity, however, because the reflection is made up of two stages; there is a "double mimesis." In the first stage, emotions are gathered, accumulated, aroused in man's inner world. These emotions are always reflections of reality. They become the basis, the material, for the second stage of reflection, where the "social-human need" brings about the imitation of those emotions. Music has its "own language," but it is not as abstract as it seems. Basic in music's "language" is rhythm, which is a factor of the objective world, but most importantly a factor in all of man's interactions with the objective world. In music, rhythm imitates the events, and tune and harmony are mimetic expressions of the feelings accompanying the events (II, 319). The main distinguishing factor of musical reflection is that the external world never appears directly (as it does in all other arts), only indirectly, as special coloring, as emphasis of emotional contents (II, 351). Finally, the aesthetic effect (catharsis) of music is more vehement and irresistible than that of other arts, but its long-range effect on ethical categories is lesser.

In Lukács' aesthetic terminology the term "realism," when applied to literature (especially novel and drama), is synonymous with his conception of "aesthetic reflection." Lukács does not see the problem of realism as "bourgeois aesthetics saw it, that realism is *one* style among many."[11] Realism did not make its first appearance in the nineteenth century (although some of its

[11] "A müvészet mint felépitmény," p. 12.

greatest representatives, Dickens, Goethe, Balzac, Tolstoy, Chekhov, Dostoyevsky, and Gogol created their works in that period); it has always been the "style" of art, whether in Homer, Aeschylus, Sophocles, Dante, Molière, or Shakespeare. In short, realistic art, and only realistic art, is worthy of being called art. The surfacing of influential "departures from realism" is not an exclusively twentieth-century phenomenon either; the history of literature is full of them. Lukács mentions the Romans, Virgil and Horace, medieval drama, and most of the representatives of French neo-classicism and German romanticism among such "departures."

Lukács' main criticism, the body of which serves as a negative definition of realism, is of the twentieth-century flood of anti-realistic literature, all of which he lists under the category of "modernism." Among the most important characteristics of "modernist" literature that he finds anti-realistic (and for that reason often anti-humanistic) are extreme and arbitrary subjectivity, distortion without a point of reference, the portrayal of "pure" essences or allegorically projected abstractions, undue emphasis upon the phenomenal, mysticism, and the incomplete, even "crippled" portrayal of man. The list should suggest that the body of literature extensively criticized includes not only ephemeral artistic trends and vogues, such as dadaism or surrealism, but also major and significant styles, including naturalism, expressionism, existentialist literature, and the so called absurd. He believes that between naturalism, on the one extreme, hopelessly mired in the particulars of phenomena, working with the surfaces of the "directly sensed" external world, and art for art's sake, on the other extreme, considering itself independent of reality, much of modern art is out of touch with the requirement of true artistic reflection: "In place of the real search for essences enters a game of chasing surface analogies, such analogies, however, which are just as abstracted from reality as the essence-portrayals of the idealist classics; on these empty constructions they then hang naturalistic, impressionistic, etc., details, and some mystifying 'world view' holds together in mock-unity the organically disparate parts."[12] The problem with the artists of "modernism," according to Lukács, is that they are unable to see correctly the relationship between essence and phenomenon, seeing them only as opposites, exclusives, or rigid contradictions. The recognition by the artist that their relationship is dialectical and that both are part of objective reality, rather than being mere products of the human consciousness, is a primary requisite of realistic art.

While expressionists, particularly German expressionists (e.g., Kaiser and Hasenclever) have created something original in dramatic structure and dialogue, Lukács believes that the overall substance of their works is extremely abstract. More than any other single factor, expressionistic works indicate their creators' alienation from society, from the real social problems, because they do not perceive the connections and relationships of the various elements in society.[13] Lukács sees as evidence of their superficial abstractions the tendency of their works to assume the attitudes of anti-scientific "machine-wreckers." Many expressionistic works see "an anti-cultural and anti-human revolt in the development of science and technology" (II, 506), simply because their authors do not understand the basics of the relationship between man and his work. The romantic-revolutionary

[12] *Marx és Engels irodalomelmélete*, p. 146.
[13] György Lukács, *Az újabb német irodalom rövid története* (Budapest, 1946), p. 129.

fervor of their protest against the obvious ills of society and their similarly revolutionary preoccupation with formalistic innovation prevents them from also seeing (and reflecting) the concrete components of the relevant social factors.

To illustrate another side of literary abstraction, Lukács compares the treatments of death by Maeterlinck and Tolstoy. Maeterlinck's early dramas, which most frequently deal with the theme of death, lift death out of its concrete human context and treat it "purely" as an "eternal problem" of human life. And what do these dramas achieve? Lukács answers: "An occasional technically poignant portrayal of animal fear of the mere fact of death. From the point of view of the writer's art [the achievement is] pure abstraction."[14] In contrast to this, Lukács considers Tolstoy's treatment of the subject a positive example of artistic realism: "Tolstoy always portrays death in connection with the individual and social life of clearly defined men. This is why death appears in his works in different, rich, complex forms, although the animal fear of death, as a *factor* of dying, here, too, often plays a big role."[15] Though in Maeterlinck's later, longer dramas the "symbols" are enveloped in thick clouds of mysticism, their abstractness is as obvious as the abstractness of the more intellectual "symbols" of expressionistic literature.

The works of Joyce, Kafka, and Beckett also suffer from the malady of abstraction, according to Lukács, but more importantly they exemplify the "modernist" trend toward extreme subjectivism, in that they are uncontrolled expressions of the writers' inner world. In these

[14] György Lukács, A *realizmus problémái* (Budapest, 1957), p. 171.
[15] *Ibid.*

works there is an atmosphere of free experimentation, where the authors arbitrarily interfere with the lives of the characters: "The characters do not receive an autonomous life, independent of the writer."[16] This subjective atmosphere carries with it a distortion, resulting from the distorting effects of the social structure on the inner world of the authors, to the point where "they feel that their own distortions are necessary conditions of every single life" (I, 724). Lukács considers it very important that all literature "have a concept of the normal if it is to 'place' distortion correctly; that is to say, to see it *as* distortion."[17] The artist must have the ability to judge the quality of action, of character, to see contradictions and extremes clearly. In most of "modernist" literature, however, "we are invited to measure one type of distortion against another and arrive necessarily at universal distortion."[18] That is pure relativism, which Lukács rejects just as categorically as he does the empiricism of naturalistic art.

The best writers of realistic literature are not working with pure relativism, which impoverishes characterizations and thereby the entire work of art. There is an ethical content present in every work of realistic reflection, coming from the assumption that there is "inherent meaningfulness" (at least to the doer) in every human action. Lukács believes that "absence of meaning makes a mockery of action and reduces art to naturalistic description."[19] In realistic art there is a value standard of which the artist is fully conscious; he controls it without blurring the lines between his own subjective world and

[16] *Ibid.*, p. 163.
[17] Georg Lukács, *Realism in Our Time*, trans. John and Necke Mander (New York, 1964), p. 33.
[18] *Ibid.*   [19] *Ibid.*, p. 36.

the independent existence of his characters. For example, Cervantes and Shakespeare (in portraying Don Quixote and Falstaff) "know exactly when, where, and to what degree their heroes are laughable or tragic, loveable or pitiable, etc."[20] As opposed to relativists, these writers are able to portray clearly even the most delicate shades of the transitions that inform the essentials, because they can see and evaluate objectively the significance of every single feeling or action. Ibsen's *The Wild Duck*, though not an example of the other extreme, for Lukács considers it a largely successful drama by realistic standards, serves as an example of blurred focus in this regard. If the comic aspects of the characters of Gregers Werle (whom Lukács sees as a Don Quixote of "idealistic demands") and Relling were clearly pointed and emphasized, rather than waveringly and hazily as Lukács believes they are, *The Wild Duck* might have been a great realistic comedy.[21] Ibsen's own uncertainty, his relativism, is reflected in the characterization, resulting in a lack of clarity.

The achievement of ethical content essential to all works of aesthetic reflection is not possible unless (as in realism) the artists view man as a "social animal" in the Aristotelian sense. In much of "modernism" (for example, in the works of Joyce, Kafka, Ionesco, and Beckett), dominated by the philosophical assumptions of existentialism, man is "by nature solitary, asocial, unable to enter into relationships with other human beings."[22] In realism, on the other hand, the characters' "ontological being," their individual existence, "cannot be distinguished from their social and historical environment.

[20] A *realizmus problémái*, p. 178.
[21] *Ibid.*, p. 179.
[22] *Realism in Our Time*, p. 20.

Their human significance, their specific individualty cannot be separated from the context in which they were created."[23] This, along with Lukács' favorable view of small detail in art, might be interpreted as a partial endorsement of naturalism and the sociological race, milieu, and moment theory of Taine. But the resemblance is only on the surface, because Lukács never encourages slavish copying of natural phenomena for its own sake; the environment (on the whole or in its details) is important to the characters and their actions only if it helps in defining them. The details should be selected for their symbolic value so that they say something far beyond what they are objectively, because the evocative power of art depends upon the use of small details that make it possible for the receivers suddenly to see and understand complex situations.[24] Nor is the selection of details restricted only to those forms actually found in objective reality. Contrary to the conclusions of ill-informed critics of Marxism, Lukács asserts that the Marxist concept of realism does allow room for our powers of imagination, that the "reflection of reality" is not in conflict with imagination-created creatures of fables, for example. The use of the fantastic may be artistically effective, because the most extreme products of our imaginations are nothing more "than such combinations, such intertwining of particular elements of reality, in ways in which we do not meet them in ordinary reality."[25]

A crucially important step in the artistic reflection of reality is the artist's careful selection of the elements (whether directly from objective reality or from imagina-

[23] *Ibid.*, p. 19.
[24] "A művészet mint felépitmény," p. 13.
[25] György Lukács, *A marxi esztétika alapjai* (Budapest, 1947), p. 11.

tion in the above sense) that make the "total" self-enclosed portrayal of some aspect of reality possible. Lukács sees the selection process as an inseparable part of the artistic perspective: "In any work of art, perspective is of overriding importance. It determines the course and content; it draws together the threads of the narration; it enables the artist to choose between the important and the superficial, the crucial and the episodic. The direction in which characters develop is determined by perspective, only those features being described which are material to their development. The more lucid the perspective—as in Molière or the Greeks—the more economical and striking the selection."[26] In Lukács' judgment, "modernism" largely ignores both selection and perspective, which brings it stylistically close to naturalism. The greatest representatives of literature with clear perspective, in addition to the Greeks and Molière, are the realists of the nineteenth century, especially Balzac, Tolstoy, Goethe, and Chekhov, and Thomas Mann of the twentieth century, whose works Lukács classifies as "critical realism." The works of these authors help to define the meaning of artistic perspective, which in Lukács' interpretation is not already existing reality but not utopia or dream either. Rather it is the objectively necessary consequence of social development, the developmental tendency of existing reality, but not something fatalistically pre-destined.[27] Perspective is not an isolated segment of a literary work (e.g., the resolution); it is an organic part of every facet of artistic portrayal. It must grow out of the real development of concrete characters. If the writer goes beyond this, his work dissolves into

[26] György Lukács, *The Meaning of Contemporary Realism*, trans. John and Necke Mander (London, 1963), p. 33.

[27] *Művészet és társadalom*, p. 301.

abstraction, and the perspective appears as an artificial decoration hung onto a natural tree.

Lukács rejects much of "socialist" literature, the Stalinist "literature as illustration," seeing in it a preference for agitation and persuasion over realistic reflection. He finds the problem primarily in the area of perspective. While he agrees that in "socialist realism" the perspective should be socialism itself, he emphasizes that socialism is a "general concept" signifying a huge period and, therefore, appearing to the individual man as an "abstract value," an "ideal."[28] If a literary work presents socialism in its abstract entirety, the perspective is overinflated and, consequently, sentimental. In socialist realism, as in all other literature, the perspective must be of modest proportions, growing out of the characters and actions of the individual work (as in Sholokhov's *The Quiet Don*), not out of the optimism or wishful thinking of the artist, because "reality, independently of thinking, independently of the writer, goes on its own way."[29] Since, in his opinion, very few works of art have been able to achieve the integration of the socialist perspective with the other requisites of aesthetic reflection, Lukács sees socialist realism as "a possibility rather than an actuality."[30] This judgment, of course, should not be taken to mean that Lukács cannot find good realistic literature written in the socialist countries. He considers Solzhenitsyn's novel, *One Day in the Life of Ivan Denisovich*, for example, an excellent work of realism.[31] That it is not socialist realism does not hurt its value as an individual work of art.

The foregoing discussion of Lukács' theory of aesthetic

[28] *Ibid.*, p. 302.   [29] *Ibid.*, p. 305.
[30] *Realism in Our Time*, p. 96.
[31] György Lukács, *Világirodalom*, II (Budapest, 1970), pp. 313-30.

reflection and realism is not complete without the content of the next chapter, dealing with Lukács' conception of the "category of specialty" in aesthetics. Lukács sees as the central aesthetic problem of realism, in the context of presenting man as a social creature, the "adequate presentation of the complete human personality,"[32] instead of "modernism's" distorted, isolated man in an abstract world. Realism means three-dimensionality, which Lukács explains through his concepts of "totality" and "type" in the context of the category of specialty. "Type" is a particularly important concept in his aesthetic theory. To avoid confusion, however, I have consciously avoided using the term in this chapter, because the meaning Lukács attaches to it is significantly different from its meaning in most other literary theory and criticism. The full discussion of "type" in the next chapter should eliminate a necessary deficiency of the present one.

[32] Georg Lukács, *Studies in European Realism* (New York, 1964), p. 7.

5.

THE CATEGORY OF SPECIALTY
IN AESTHETICS

In surveying the history of aesthetic theory,[1] Lukács
concludes that several misunderstandings and misexpla-
nations have resulted from various theorists' erroneous
concepts of categories as related to aesthetics. Some (e.g.,
Plato) have examined and evaluated art merely as epistemology, labeling it either "lie" or "illusion," while
others (e.g., Schelling, Kant, and other proponents of
"genius" theories) have categorically separated cognition
(epistemology) and artistic peculiarity, putting them at
opposite poles. Even Aristotle, whose great contribution
to aesthetics Lukács acknowledges repeatedly, is faulted
by him in this area. Aristotle, in comparing history and
poetry, recognizes only the categories of individuality and
universality. He concludes, accordingly, that poetry is of
greater significance than history because it is closer to
universality, hence, to philosophy. There is no hint of the
existence of a category special to art. Not until the eight-
eenth century, with the contributions of Diderot and
Lessing, does the groping for the special category begin.
Lukács credits Hegel with the methodological definition
of specialty as a necessary mediator between universality
and individuality, and Goethe with the realization that
the category of specialty is central to art.

[1] György Lukács, A különösség, mint esztétikai kategória
(Budapest, 1957), pp. 11-127.

71

From the positive and negative aspects of these, plus the sporadic contributions of Marxist classics (Marx, Engels, Lenin) Lukács derives a clarified explanation of the relationship of categories and achieves, in particular, a determination of the category of specialty as central in the context of his theory of artistic reflection. To Lukács, categories are not metaphysical, merely subjective products of thinking, not a static, immutable system (as with Kant); rather they are real, objective facts of reality.[2] Reality (as seen from his ontology) is not static, but a changing historical reality. As reality changes, develops, so must the categories. Categories are not reflections of reality; they are aspects of reality the mind observes and orders into concepts that reflect reality. In the area of aesthetics they are useful not to fix permanently, but to help determine, the nature of art, the art-work as an independent totality, the process and the factors involved in its creation, and to differentiate it from other human endeavors and products.

The three categories in question are: the *individual* (*das Einzelne*), the *universal* (*das Allgemeine*), and the *special* (*das Besondere*). Specialty is that category which falls between the extreme categories of individuality and universality, whose peripheries are much clearer than those of specialty. Individuality refers to the "this" of phenomena and is without any degree of generalization, while universality refers to the "all" and is the ultimate of generalization. If reality is conceived of materialistically and dialectically, then its reflection in human thinking must be in the form of striving from the individual

---

[2] György Lukács, *Az esztétikum sajátossága*, II (Budapest, 1969), p. 177. Further references to this work in this chapter will be identified parenthetically (by volume and page) in the text.

to the universal and from the universal to the individual, back to the universal, and so on.[3] (Generalizations can be derived only from the individuals, which, in turn, are better understood with the help of generalizations, and the newly illuminated individuals can lead to more accurate generalizations. The process is endless.) Along the lengthy road between the two, there are an infinite number of points of relative generalizations, which constitute (roughly) the category of specialty. The three categories have a function in all modes of reflection, but with significant differences. In science, for example, where the striving is for the most accurate generalizations (laws), the category of specialty is merely a helpful mediator, of temporary use, not in any sense a final form or goal. The goal of science is the achievement of knowledge of the "world-for-itself" for man by disanthropomorphic means. Each new scientific achievement (generalization) is built in substance upon previous ones, the new superseding the old. Art, however, is the anthropomorphic reflection of man's awareness of mankind's development, man's self-consciousness. Art's goal is not the discovery of the most accurate universals, nor a preoccupation with the isolated individual, though it does not ignore either one. The territory where art-works take their final form is somewhere between the two, in the category of specialty. For this reason, a new work of art is not built in substance upon previous ones, though it uses the accumulated methodological achievements of previous artists; and it does not supersede previous ones, rather, it is essentially original, created from scratch.

Lukács' dialectical materialism, in disagreement with Aristotle and Hegel, holds that "universalization is never

---

[3] A különösség, mint esztétikai kategória, p. 91.

the autonomous end-point of thinking."[4] The universal is the essence of the individual, but it only "approximately" holds together its individual members, never fully representing them.[5] Lukács believes that neither of these, alone, is adequate for artistic expression (hence, his rejection of naturalism, allegory, abstract art, and the art of "pure essences"). The dynamic-dialectical unity of the two is achieved in the category of specialty, which contains elements of each, and in a certain sense, especially as a means of artistic reflection, is superior to both. Moreover, specialty, when represented in a finished, individual work of art, is a category independent of both universality and individuality. Specialty is not merely a relative universalization, nor a "road from the individual to the universal" (as in science); rather it is a "necessary mediation between the individual and the universal" (II, 180). In life we come into direct contact with the individual, but it is impossible fully to understand, think, and communicate this without the help of the universal, and the reverse is equally true. The category of specialty is the area where the dialectical "elimination-preservation" (II, 226) of universality, on the one hand, and individuality, on the other, occurs. Thus, it contains both, but it is neither.

There is a similarity between art and ethics. The ethical middle in Hegel (and also in Aristotle) stands between subjective morality (*Moralität*) and objective law (*Recht*). Lukács' view is that the ethical middle is not the exact center (Aristotle), but a mediatory center (Hegel), achieving a synthesis of the two extremes. Specialty in ethics is a "field," not a rigidly fixed mean, allowing movement to correct the errors of the individual act

[4] *Ibid.*, p. 85.   [5] *Ibid.*, p. 90.

and the purely objective law. The difference between ethics and aesthetics is that while ethics concerns itself only with the good, with positive examples, and is paradigmatic, aesthetics contains in itself the good and the bad, the positive and the negative with equal force, and it is much less paradigmatic. Nevertheless, in art, as in ethics, the category of specialty as "mediatory center" is also a "field," an "in between segment of the road, a space for movement, an area" (II, 235). The "movement" is from the center to the peripheries of the two extreme categories, leaving, in principle, much room for operation, excluding only those works which function merely in the extremes of the universal (e.g., allegory) and the individual (e.g., naturalism), or those which contain both, but only side by side, never achieving a synthesis.

As far as the individual art-work is concerned, its center may be fixed anywhere within this "space for movement." Its position is influenced by art forms, genres, styles, and individual artists. For example: "Drama conceives its figures and situations much more universally than the epic; in it, the traits of individuality enter much less frequently, in much less detail; in drama every individual detail has a symbolic-symptomatic emphasis, which is the characteristic of the epic only to a much smaller degree."[6] Further, within the genre of drama, Racine's plays are closer to the universal than Shakespeare's, while modern bourgeois drama is even closer to the individual. These differences in no way imply any necessary deficiency among the various styles, genres, or authors. Nor do they imply prescribed rules and laws (for example, that all works of drama must always be closer to the universal than any work of epic). Lukács

[6] *Ibid.*, p. 135.

75

believes that aesthetic laws are present only in the body of accumulated works and that they are "reborn, expanded, concretized" with every new work of art.[7]

Among those factors influential on the individual artwork, the subjective being of the individual artist and the question of originality deserve separate discussion. With regard to the former, Lukács not only rejects every "genius" theory, he even rejects Zola's theory that the artistic "temperament" is an unavoidable coloring factor in the final artistic product. The particular from which the artist starts is his own self, his individuality, with his own convictions and prejudices. If the core of his artwork, however, is primarily his own subjective being, if he generalizes directly from this, then he never enters the aesthetic realm—the special. The artist can arrive from his individuality to the aesthetic generalization, the special, only by way of coming into touch with objective reality, only by striving for the "faithful, true reflection of reality."[8] Balzac is a clear illustration of this principle, because in his personal views he was always a conservative-royalist, yet his novels were not generalizations of these views but the truthful artistic reflections of the reality of his time. Engels called the case of Balzac "the triumph of realism," and Lukács frequently cites it as the prime example of the correct artistic attitude and method.

What, then, is the source of artistic originality? Lukács sees the artist's originality mainly in the forming of an art-work. True, it is of primary importance that the artist be able to "grasp the essentially new contents of his age," but he is original only if he also succeeds in creating "for this new content an organically adequate, newly born

[7] *Ibid.*, p. 138.   [8] *Ibid.*, p. 166.

form."[9] The original artist grasps the essence of each new phenomenon, but instead of revealing it as a mere generalization, he shapes it into a work that is the special destiny of special men. He shapes it in such a way that the essence is completely "dissolved" in the phenomenon, rather than appearing as a separate entity in the work of art: "There is before us a world, which seemingly consists merely of phenomena, but such phenomena, which, without losing their forms as phenomena . . . make the essences hidden in the phenomena experienceable, evocative."[10]

Only the completed work of art exists fully in that particular state of being Lukács calls specialty. It is created by man and does not claim to be reality in the sense of objective reality. Yet it stands before us as "reality," because our thoughts, desires, cannot change its existence; we must accept it as it is; we can only approve or reject its reality subjectively. Though we cannot interfere with it (as we can with objective reality), it can affect us because it is evocative, its reality is sensuous, for the elimination of its direct individuality is also a preservation of it (unlike in science). The elevation of the individual to the level of the special means that the artistic generalization is made to reside (in a dissolved form) in every detail as well as the totality of the art-work, making it quite unlike any particular segment of objective reality, rather, a world of its own that, nevertheless, is a reflection of the essential connections, of the forms of the phenomena of objective reality.[11]

The category of specialty is the central category of aesthetics, because only through its governance can art evoke a "world" that is typical and total. Specialty, then,

[9] *Ibid.*, p. 171.   [10] *Ibid.*, p. 184.   [11] *Ibid.*, pp. 141-42.

is "the structural essence of aesthetics" (II, 177). The evocation of a "world" directed to affect the subjective being of the receiver is unique to the artistic mode of reflection: "The aesthetic object's . . . aesthetic peculiarity is in the fact that the mimesis, with the help of the peculiar mode of reflection of objective reality, evokes certain experiences in the receiver's subjective being. If we disregard this, the aesthetic formation as such ceases to exist; it remains a block of stone, a piece of canvas, an object which is the same as all other objects, and as such, existing independently of any consciousness, subjectivity. Therefore, the thesis, that no object exists without the subjective, refers exclusively to the aesthetic nature of such formations" (I, 515). The world evoked, moreover, is able to present an intensive totality only if governed by the category of specialty, and the creation of the typical (which, like specialty, is a synthesis fundamental to realistic art) is possible only in the context of the special category.

The Notion of Type

It should be noted at the outset that Lukács is not talking about the simple type, the superficial type, the stereotype marked merely by so many conventional, external characteristics. Nor is he talking about the permanent type in which the essential (universal) is an eternal-final quality, the individual being just a token dressing up of this in sensuous form. Rather, he attempts to define a type in art that is pluralistic: one in which each example is three-dimensional, different from all other examples, and each broadens and enriches the universal determination of that type. Lukács' description of type is closely linked with his theory of the accumulative quality of the aesthetic effect in the receiver,[12] in terms of man's awareness of his historical development, especially ethically.

Since Lukács' critical writings make extensive use of the concept of type, giving many specific illustrations, it is possible to begin here with a negative definition, with an explanation and exemplification of what type is not. Once again, the negative examples come from naturalism and what he calls "modernism." First, type is not the ordinary, the average. For explanation he offers this example: "Let us take such a representative modern writer as Dos Passos. He describes, for example, a debate about capitalism and socialism. The room where the debate occurs receives an excellent, lively sketch. We can see the smoky Italian restaurant with its tomato-stained tablecloth, the tri-colored remains of the melted ice cream on the plate, etc. The particular speech and tone of each individual participant of the discussion is also well hit upon by the writer. But what they say is complete banality, it is that average pro and con which can be found any time, any place, in any conversation of philistines."[13] If the poet conceives of the age and its great problems in depth, his portrayal of it will not be on an everyday, ordinary level. In everyday life the contradictions are dulled; they appear indifferently as "disjointed accidents," never receiving a truly clear form, which can happen only if the contradiction reaches its most extreme, most ultimate consequences, if "everything contained in it becomes perceptible and obvious."[14] Lukács considers naturalism the greatest advocate of this average, indifferent banality. But he also contends that

[12] See Chapter VIII.
[13] György Lukács, *Művészet és társadalom* (Budapest, 1968), p. 156.
[14] *Ibid.*, p. 144.

the "extreme subjectivism" of much of "modernism," despite its appearance to the contrary, fails to escape the average: "The experiments, which came into existence during the seemingly fervent struggle against naturalism, to portray the 'extraordinary' man, the eccentric man, even the 'superman,' remain within that same magic-circle which starts with the naturalist movement. In both life and art, the eccentric man, the individual 'isolated' from everyday reality and the average man are poles which amplify and complement each other."[15] He adds that the superman and the philistine are equally empty, equally distant from the deep social conflicts and every true content of history: "Both are faint, abstract, narrow, one-sided, ultimately inhuman phenomena."[16]

The typical, then, is neither the average, the mathematical mean, not the eccentric; in fact it is not a fixed point at all, whether in the extremes or the center. The typical has a range equal to the "space for movement" of the category of specialty. It is a key concept in Lukács' aesthetics for the determination of those elements (action, situation, character, etc.), which best mediate the individual (e.g., the historical "here and now") and the universal (e.g., the essential, although not in the metaphysical sense). In creating the typical the artist embodies in the destinies of certain concrete men the most important characteristics of some historical situation that best represent the specific age, nation, and class to which they belong.[17] The result of this mediation of the individual and the universal preserves and deepens both, so that the type is more and better (aesthetically) than either or both separately. As an illustration, Lukács quotes painter

[15] *Ibid.*, pp. 151-52.   [16] *Ibid.*, p. 152.
[17] György Lukács, "A művészet mint felépitmény" (a special publication of the Hungarian Cultural Ministry, 1955), p. 15.

80

Max Liebermann's quip: "My painting of you is more like you than you are" (II, 227).

Lukács is aware that one of the most difficult problems for the artist is the avoidance of the portrayal of the "typical as such," because the typical, falling within the broad category of specialty, is in itself a degree of universalization. The art-work, however, if it is to succeed in evoking a world that affects the receiver's subjective being, must portray concrete men, in concrete situations, expressing concrete feelings.[18] If it only succeeds in creating a typical that is recognizable as such, the result is still just an abstraction of human life, tossing formlessly and homelessly between the conceptual and the evocative. The problem, however, does not lead back to naturalism, which does not go beyond the correct observation of everyday reality. For the great poet this observation is only the beginning, the important raw material. The poet's understanding of life consists in that based upon his grasp of the essential characteristics he both organizes these elements of reality and "*invents* such situations and characters, which are wholly impossible in everyday life,"[19] but are capable of clearly revealing (as opposed to their muddy quality in life) the forces, struggles, and contradictions of life (e.g., Don Quixote). Marxist aesthetic theory, continues Lukács, "does not prescribe slavish adherence to the facts of everyday life . . . its average phenomena, it does not exclude the imagination, the fantasy."[20] Art should be "momentous and interesting."[21] It achieves this double goal through the creation of the typical in which the universal truth (the "momentous")

[18] A *különösség, mint esztétikai kategória*, p. 218.

[19] *Művészet és társadalom*, p. 144.

[20] György Lukács, A *marxi esztétika alapjai* (Budapest, 1947), p. 15.

[21] *Ibid.*, p. 12.

is "dissolved" in the individual (the "interesting" and "evocative") without destroying its individuality for a single moment.

This determination of the typical in art refers us back to Lukács' explanation of the category of specialty and the rational function of the creative artist who shapes the form of the art-work in such a way that it "seemingly consists merely of phenomena," but, in fact, its "hidden essences" are "experienceable, evocative" in the phenomena (e.g., the destinies of concrete men). This constitutes the "symbolic-symptomatic" nature of art as well as its "paradigmatic" quality. Lukács is cautious, however, with the use of the term "paradigmatic," because it is potentially capable of creating a confusion between ethics and aesthetics. (He points out, for example, that the Stalinist dogma that considers artists the "engineers of the soul" is the result of such confusion, expecting artists simply to exemplify "good" ethical behavior of "socialist men.") While he regards the ethical content of art as very important and realizes that the creation of the typical makes "every action portrayed more-or-less paradigmatic," he clarifies the differences by stressing that the aesthetic paradigm "contains everything negative, everything that wavers between good and bad, while exemplification in the ethical sense must always be something essentially positive" (II, 541). The artistic work does not serve out examples to follow or "Thou shalt nots," but it does contain, through the typical and the artistic perspective, "inherent" judgments about "how much and in what way does this kind of man, this kind of destiny advance or impede the constant development of mankind."[22]

[22] "A művészet mint felépitmény," p. 12.

Lukács finds it necessary to emphasize repeatedly that his aesthetic theories are fully consistent with those of the Marxist classics. He is aware that some of his critics, despite his professedly Marxist "late" works, have placed him "within the tradition of German idealism."[23] The concept of the typical appears to be one of the most important areas of his aesthetics, where he can show evidence of a strong link with Marx and Engels. There are, however, occasional unresolved contradictions. For example, Lukács quotes with approval Engels' statement that "in my view, by realism we understand, beside the truth of details, the reflection of typical characters in typical circumstances."[24] In agreeing with this, Lukács seems to forget his rejection of the "truth of details" as such, in connection with his criticism of Plato and of naturalism. More importantly, however, Marx, Engels, and Lukács are in complete agreement when it comes to citing the best concrete examples of literary realism and the typical: "Marx and Engels saw in Shakespeare and Balzac (in contrast, say, to Schiller on the one, and Zola on the other side) that artistic, that realistic direction, which best satisfied their aesthetic theories."[25] Lukács regards Shakespeare as the best historical dramatist because of his superb creation of typical characters and conflicts, even without a sense of history available to nineteenth- and twentieth-century writers. He says, in unison with Engels, that "Shakespeare is the greatest, the unsurpassable example of realistic literature."[26]

[23] George Lichtheim, *George Lukács* (New York, 1970), p. 140.

[24] György Lukács, *Marx és Engels irodalomelmélete* (Budapest, 1949), p. 112.

[25] *Ibid.*, p. 149.   [26] *Ibid.*, p. 112.

Totality in Art

In Lukács' philosophy the term "totality" does not refer to a rigidly fixed, static quantity. He distinguishes between "extensive" and "intensive" totalities, both of which are infinite. Any mode of reflection can only hope to achieve closer and closer approximations of totality, not to conquer it, know it conclusively. The "extensive" and "intensive" totalities are not only infinite in their characteristics, but are also changing, developing. This is so in social reality: "Human society is a unified historical development, every manifestation, every action of human life being part of this historical development. That is: art, science, recreation, family life, etc., make up a unity which is in constant transformation."[27] Now, art is a "social phenomenon" and as such it reflects neither the private, the individual, nor the universal (abstract, even transcendental) reality, but, governed by the category of specialty, it reflects the dynamic-typical, historical reality. The social-historical context is the key element of all artistic (realistic) reflection.

In view of this, Lukács fights against two "false" conceptions of totality: (1) that art reflects the universal human condition, and (2) that every particular part of an art-work must satisfy the corresponding particulars of reality, that it be a copy of a segment of life. The first of these is exemplified by works of "modernism" whose philosophical basis is existentialism. These works, he believes, inflate either the individual artists' "alienation" from capitalist society or the crippling factors (e.g., technology, division of labor) of capitalist society that seriously affect man's totality, into an eternal, permanent, universal *condition humaine*. The problem is that the

[27] A *marxi esztétika alapjai*, p. 3.

artists' own "crippled" state, their alienation, their iso-
lation, prevents them from seeing the real social connections, from asking the relevant questions, for example:
"How, in whose hands, will the powers of civilization
become anti-cultural?"[28] Their works, therefore, are not
the universal, total pictures they purport to be. The second conception of totality Lukács combats is both new
and old. It includes Plato's insistence upon comparing
the details of art to the details of reality, the Renaissance theory of verisimilitude, as well as naturalist efforts
to make art scientific. This conception does not recognize that the individual art-work is a "self-enclosed
entity"; it drags external elements into its construction
and evaluation.

What, then, is the correct conception of totality in
art, as viewed by Lukács? First, let us briefly return to
Lukács' thoughts on "extensive" and "intensive" totalities. "Extensive" totality includes all elements of objective reality, whether or not they are of any significant
concern to man. The limits of this are far beyond the
possibilities of art; only the sciences are capable of reflecting its infinite processes with growing approximation.
"Intensive" totality is the depth of "man's totality" (*der
Mensch ganz*), but, very importantly, man in the full
context of interaction with the relevant elements of his
social-historical environment. This, too, is infinite, so
that artistic portrayal of it is only an approximation. Still,
Lukács believes, instead of chasing "extensive" totality,
art's concern and priority should be "the achievement of
depth, of intensive totality."[29]

This description of totality in art takes us back to the

[28] György Lukács, *Lenin* (Budapest, 1970), p. 150.
[29] Georg Lukács, *Realism in Our Time*, trans. John and Necke
Mander (New York, 1964), p. 100.

creation of the typical. The intensive depth of man's totality is achieved through typical characters (in typical actions and situations) who, without losing their concrete, individual forms, contain in themselves the richness and depth of all the relevant social processes of their time and circumstances. The characters run the complete course of their personal destinies and finish it off in concretely defined circumstances (the historical "here and now"). The work of art, thus, is a self-enclosed total entity, different from other modes of reflection and different from reality, though it appears to us as reality independent of our consciousness, affecting our hopes, desires, sympathies, etc., while we, in turn, cannot affect it. The art-work's form is total and final.

By concretely defined circumstances, the historical "here and now" in which the typical characters run the course of their destinies, Lukács does not mean the kind of historicity found in Renaissance theory. Once again, Shakespeare serves as example: "As a true dramatist Shakespeare does not try to paint a detailed picture of historical and social circumstances. He characterizes the period through his actors."[30] In drama, the typical characterizations are the mediators of all other relevant factors: "Shakespeare showed titanically how great historical collisions could be translated into human terms and imbued with dramatic life."[31] Lukács clearly prefers the authenticity of the essential social-historical atmosphere to a simple historical authenticity. He considers Macbeth an excellent drama of "the disintegration of feudal society," of the "class struggle between monarchy and feudalism."[32] Lukács believes that in portraying the es-

[30] Georg Lukács, The Historical Novel, trans. Hannah and Stanley Mitchell (London, 1962), p. 118.
[31] Ibid., p. 137.   [32] Ibid.

86

sence of this struggle, through the creation of typical characters and situations functioning in their "own world," Shakespeare was entirely correct in altering many small historical details. For example, he disagrees with Hegel's suggestion that Shakespeare should have included Macbeth's rightful claim to the Scottish throne as a motive because the source had mentioned it. Lukács thinks it would have been superfluous in light of the more typical arbitrary use of such claims in the struggles of feudalistic societies.

In the final analysis, then, the concepts of the "total" and the "typical" are found to form an inseparable unity in Lukács' aesthetics. Reality, as we know it in everyday life, is by no means falsified through the art-work's independent "own world"; rather, it is heightened. The "dissolution" of the essential in the individual, creating the typical, brings to us a sharper, more complete picture of reality than we otherwise possess. Such a complete artistic picture is richer, deeper, and more meaningful than the particular and the exceptional, even if the latter are historically authentic. Only such an artistic picture can evoke an aesthetic effect in the receiver, which is the reason for its being as "social phenomenon."

6.

THE LANGUAGE OF ART

Lukács approaches this subject from the broader context of the languages of human life. He distinguishes among three human signalizing systems that may be involved in any mode of reflection or communication. The earliest and most basic of these is what he calls the *primary signalizing system*. This is roughly the equivalent of the Pavlovian "conditioned reflex," which gives birth to and supports the two more advanced systems. The most abstract of the three is the *secondary signalizing system*. This is what we commonly think of as *the* language we possess, in which we think and speak. The secondary signalizing system is quite drastically separated from the primary signalizing system (by its abstraction) but continues to rely upon it indirectly. It is a separate and independent means of reflection and communication. The third system, which Lukács calls the *primary plus signalizing system*, is somewhere between the other two, similar to the position of the category of specialty in relation to the individual and the universal. However, the primary plus signalizing system is more than just a combination of various parts of the other two systems. In fact, it can achieve a synthesis which is capable of rising far above the limitations of the other two. It is the primary plus signalizing system that Lukács designates as the language of art, by means of which art (especially poetry) is "capable of expressing what is otherwise inexpressible."[1]

[1] György Lukács, *Az esztétikum sajátossága*, ii (Budapest,

Both signalizing systems of the higher order are considerably more complicated, more abstract, and less direct than the primary system. These characteristics, however, make it possible for them to communicate more about both the internal and external worlds of man, in a deeper, richer, more extensive, more comprehensive way (II, 59). The secondary system is most appropriate for making generalizations, while the primary plus system is capable of individualizing, as well as generalizing, thereby serving as the primary instrument for the understanding of man. Lukács stresses that the primary plus signalizing system is a rational language, though it is not purely on the level of thinking (as is the secondary system) and some of its contents are not possible to verbalize. It has several special qualities that the others (primary and secondary) do not have, but irrationality is not one of them.

The question that must necessarily be asked here is: how does Lukács treat intuition and the unconscious in this connection? The answer is that intuition and the unconscious are parts of the primary plus signalizing system (and of the secondary signalizing system) but only in terms of Lukács' definition of those concepts. His definition of intuition is influenced by Pavlov's materialistic psychology. Intuition, says Lukács, "contrary to modern irrational philosophy from Schelling to Bergson, is not a higher form of perception of reality" (II, 38). It is not something higher and it is not something other than rational. Rather than being a higher perception of reality, intuition is a sudden perception (realization) of some essential connection, relationship, without consciousness of the details of the process that led to the conclusion.

1969), p. 175. Further references to this work in this chapter will be identified parenthetically (by volume and page) in the text.

One remembers the result, but not the road that led to it. The important point is that the process is nevertheless rational. A simple example may be a tennis player's adjustment to a certain game situation that seems purely reflexive-intuitive on the surface, but only years of careful conditioning, methodical learning, and practice can make his response consistently correct. Afterwards, though it may take a long time, it is always possible to describe (rationally) what the probable elements were that led to his reflexive-intuitive reaction.

The Kantian unconscious receives the same treatment from Lukács as does intuition. Lukács does not recognize a metaphysical separation between conscious and unconscious thinking and knowledge. Intuition and the unconscious are completions of the conscious, with which they are constantly interacting. There are many processes that occur predominantly in the unconscious. Memory, or the process of recall, is an example: "No human being would be capable of thought and action if everything that he is capable of recalling at appropriate times would be constantly present in his consciousness" (II, 124). There is no difference, then, between the contents of the conscious and the unconscious; in the thinking process the same contents fluctuate from one to the other. At one time or another, everything the mind possesses has been in the consciousness. With these qualifications, intuition and the unconscious can be part of the primary plus signalizing system without destroying its rationality. They are, thus, a part of the process of artistic creation, helping to make it a "peculiar," extremely complex, and "decidedly teleological activity" (II, 135).

Lukács' determination of the primary plus signalizing system is best approached by way of the examples he gives. The first set of examples consists of those aural-visual elements which are changed from the primary system to the level of the primary plus system (in everyday use and in art), providing the individuality of the expression. In the case of speech, the subtext—the meaning between the lines and accompanying the lines—is of great significance. Gestures, facial expressions, intonations, stresses, pauses, etc., which may reinforce, contradict, color, but always individualize the meaning of the abstract words, "are often of greater significance from the point of view of understanding content, than the meaning of the actual words" (II, 49). Equally significant are the first impressions (correct or incorrect) because they invariably influence any subsequent communication. In his practical criticism, Lukács often points to the artistic value of silences. He believes that "every silence has its own color, atmosphere" (II, 63) from which its unique, individual meaning can be understood. He cites Strindberg's short play *The Stronger*, in which only one of the two characters speaks, and certain key scenes of *Miss Julie* as successful examples of the dramatic use of silence. In one scene of *Miss Julie* the heroine tries unsuccessfully to persuade Kristin to run off with her and Jean. About this Lukács remarks: "Strindberg solves the problem before him with exquisite skill. He expresses the heroine's hope, effort and failure merely through the tempo of her speech, while the other character makes no protest, only her silence influences the tempo of the speech."[2]

Laughter, as an expression, is also an extremely important part of the primary plus signalizing system, although some instances of laughter are reflexive reactions. Laughter resulting from tickling, for example, is an uncondi-

[2] György Lukács, *Művészet és társadalom* (Budapest, 1968), p. 157.

tioned reflex reaction, while the laughter aroused by factors such as unconventional appearance or diction (resulting from "social prejudices") belongs to the category of conditioned reflexes. But most instances of laughter are on a level higher than simple reflexes, in the category of the primary plus signalizing system. As such "laughter is a universal means of expression" (II, 61) capable of communicating the giant scale of human feelings, convictions, attitudes, etc., such as sincerity, slyness, naiveté, cunning, inhibition, openness—in fact, so many shades of these and others that abstract language is not equipped to describe them adequately. It is Lukács' conviction that through the process of civilization and humanization the *individual* characteristics of the subjects of laughter have increased in number to the point that they dominate—but do not eliminate—the typical (II, 61).

Another primarily aural example of the primary plus signalizing system is crying. Like laughter, crying is also capable of innumerable shades of expression; therefore it too is individualizing. Crying and laughter can be part of mood, an aural-visual blend and a complex example of the primary plus signalizing system. It is regarded by Lukács as a very important means of expression in all arts. Here Lukács stresses the importance of the use of details, their selection, symbolic value, and arrangement. Slightly different arrangements of the same set of objects in the same environment, for example, can sometimes create drastically different moods, and the changing of a few words in a spoken sentence can do the same without altering its basic content. Mood, of course, is part of the content, but it is an imperceptible part. What Lukács is saying, in fact, is that mood is the one element of the primary plus signalizing system that comes close to communicating directly to the unconscious of the receiver: "Ordinarily, mood can develop only if it does not come to light; something that has a perceivable mood, often has a sobering, even comical effect" (II, 65). The arrangement is conscious, but the unity of mood must seem accidental in an art-work; it should not be seen as mood.

In these and other examples of the primary plus signalizing system "every signal relates to the subjective and strives to evoke" (II, 110-11). An essential distinguishing factor of the primary plus signalizing system is that only the readiness necessary for production and reception can be learned. There is no comparatively simple one-to-one relationship between sign and object as in abstract language (the secondary system) that could be simply memorized. But the above illustrations exemplify only one side of the primary plus signalizing system, the side transformed from the level of conditioned reflexes, the primary system. The other side consists of the transformation of the secondary signalizing system, of the denotative meaning of abstract language.

While science strives to deanthropomorphize language (the secondary system) in order to make it objective and precisely logical, to fix exact denotative meanings in a one-to-one relationship between sign and object as much as possible, the primary language of art (poetry) exploits and expands its many shades and meanings, preserving, however, language's denotative capacity, its ability to reflect objective reality (II, 153). The many meanings include essentially everything beyond the denotative meanings of words and word combinations (the emotional, the ambiguous, the associative, the sensuous emphasis, etc.), that constitute the "magic" of words. The utilization of the "magic" of words is the exploitation by art of the anthropomorphic use of the secondary signalizing system. The anthropomorphic use of language in everyday life means that man does not use words to describe an object for the sake of the object; "on the contrary, this has always been linked with a definite human attitude, and only in this relationship did it become interesting and significant" (II, 167). The difference between the everyday use of "anthropomorphic language" (the secondary system transformed into the primary plus) and the poetic use is that, while in everyday use the many meanings, the "magic," is random, accidental, simultaneously effective and ineffective, in poetry the infinite shades of meanings are used selectively (conscious selection), only the relevant aspects of the total connotative potential of the words being pointed, emphasized in any particular context. Thus its use in poetry is clear, rather than random and confusing as in life. If it is confusing in poetry, then it has been either unable to surpass everyday language or is intentionally obscure; in either case the result is not art.

Lukács reminds us again that "art and artistic sensitivity were not born with mankind" (II, 108); on the contrary, they are the products of a long social-historical development. The origin and the development of the primary plus signalizing system is the result of this process. It has developed to the point where it is capable of functioning relatively independently of the other two systems. (Lukács gives a long analysis—II, 75-89—of three "pathological" cases, Strindberg, Van Gogh, and Hölderlin, to prove this thesis.) This "relative independence" is similar to that of the category of specialty, in that the primary plus signalizing system is a dialectical synthesis, the "preservation-elimination" of the other two systems. It is capable of being both conceptual and sensuous, rational and evocative, objective and subjective, universal and individual, at the same time. The effective synthesis in the primary plus signalizing system of these apparent dualities can be illustrated through the dramas of Chekhov: "Chekhov builds his dramas on the contradictions between his characters' subjective intentions and objective directions and their significance. For this reason, the viewer constantly finds himself in a double-edged situation, because he understands and sympathizes with the characters' feelings, but at the same time he is forced to live through the tragic, tragicomic, or comic contradictions between the subjective feelings and the society's objective reality just as intensely" (II, 171). In light of this, Lukács believes that Brecht, in proposing the "alienation effect," is "banging on open doors," because in its method of portrayal drama already achieves an alienation effect, which is precisely what makes it drama and why it needs no additional "alienation effect" in the Brechtian sense (II, 171). The important point is that the conceptual and the sensuous, the universal and individual, etc., do not appear side by side or alternately in a work of art. The primary plus signalizing system, functioning in harmony with the category of specialty, makes it possible for these elements to appear to the receiver in an integrated form, in a synthesis.

ALLEGORY AND SYMBOLISM

Lukács' discussion of allegory and symbolism is tightly linked with the concepts of specialty, type, this-worldliness, realism (reflection), and language (the primary plus signalizing system). He does recognize that allegory is a form belonging to aesthetics, but he does not consider it wholly adequate: "We may discuss allegory within aesthetics as one—though problematic—forming style, be-

cause despite its many anti-artistic tendencies it brings
about a sensuously homogeneous picture of reality. The
individual and the abstract universal, of course, are connected by it in a worldless, abstract manner, which can
be of lasting effect only as contentless decoration" (II,
691-92). Lukács' preference is clearly for symbolism, but
he knows that the borderlines between the two are hazily
drawn by most aesthetic theories. Since he finds allegory
a major formalistic principle in "modernist" literature
(see *Realism in Our Time*) he considers it important to
differentiate between allegory and symbolism. His starting point is Goethe's definition, founded in Hegelian aesthetics: "It makes a big difference whether the poet seeks
the special to fit the universal, or contemplates the universal in the special. In the first case allegory comes into
being, where the special is valid only as a paradigm of
the universal. But the second case is really the nature of
poetry: it expresses the special, without thinking of, or
referring to the universal. Now, whoever grasps the living
image of this special, also grasps the universal with it,
without realizing it, or realizing it only later."[3] It is easy
to see how the second of these methods (symbolism)
resembles dialectical materialism in terms of cognition,
while the form of allegory is akin to idealism, for it works
with the assumption of the primacy of the essence and
the dualistic separation of essence and phenomenon. The
"content" of allegory, so long as its starting point is the
universal, is really best expressed in conceptual language;
particularization through allegorical images only impoverishes it (serving as illustration at best), because the
particular and the universal do not achieve a synthesis.
Symbolism, on the other hand, starts with the par-

[3] Goethe, *Maximen und Reflexionen*, as quoted by Lukács,
Az esztétikum sajátossága, II, p. 676.

ticular phenomenon of objective reality and its corresponding essence (idea) found in the phenomenon, changing them (by means of the primary plus signalizing system) into a synthetic picture in such an effective manner that both are preserved. This synthesis of the individual and the universal is the category of specialty, the central category of aesthetics.

The objection might be raised that much of Lukács' argument against allegory is not properly in the realm of art, but in philosophical and theological basic assumptions. If one believes in the existence of a higher reality that transcends the objective, physical reality (whether it is called the world of ideas, forms or noumenal world) and concludes (with Schlegel and Schiller) that the artistic genius is best equipped, through intuition or inspiration, to look into this world (otherwise inconceivable) and project it through the medium of his art by making it sensuous and perceivable in the chosen allegorical images, then one finds the method rejected by Goethe and Lukács fully adequate. Lukács does not, however, argue against the validity of the idealistic world view here; he simply points out the this-worldliness and anthropocentric qualities of artistic reflection. Allegory denies these; therefore it is not art in Lukács' definition.

The differences between symbolism and allegory, as seen by Lukács, might be well illustrated if we look at the dramas of Maeterlinck and Chekhov. Maeterlinck's symbolism (allegory to Lukács) grows out of an abstract, transcendental world and remains an effective illustration (e.g., in terms of mood) of mystical-transcendental powers. The human beings (e.g., in *Pélléas and Mélisande*) are portrayed as little more than one-dimensional puppets. In works like *The Blue Bird* and *The Intruder*, the "symbols" are more conceptual and beg to be given

97

abstract labels. In Lukács' judgment such works are "totally contentless ornamental forms, which only through their geometric essences, geometric combinations, arrive at independent, 'contentless,' abstract contents" (II, 679). In contrast to this, Chekhov's art is this-worldly, its symbolism growing out of objective reality in context of the "world" of the plays. Particulars (such as the cherry orchard, Moscow, etc.), retain their individuality while growing into symbols expressing universality as well. They are not translatable into abstract language (need not be) and are effective as symbols only in the individual art-work in which they appear as synthetic parts.

What, we may ask, is the case if the symbolic elements in a work of art seem to be obviously "other-worldly" figures like the gods of Greek tragedy? Lukács is ready to answer this; in fact he emphasizes that the contrasting of allegorical and symbolic artistic methods is nowhere more appropriate than in "the most typical phenomenon of mimesis: the formation of the naked and tragic man" (II, 692). He compares the basic situations of Agamemnon-Iphigenia and Abraham-Isaac, because in both cases the conflict is resolved by the interference of a higher power, and, in both cases, the issue is the sacrifice of a child by the father to a god. Lukács agrees with Kierkegaard's conclusion that there is a radical difference between the contents of the two cases. Kierkegaard's conviction is that "the tragic hero remains within the ethical."[4] In direct contrast to Abraham, whose motive is personal virtue in context of a private relationship with a transcendental god, "Agamemnon must sacrifice his daughter for the happiness of all

[4] S. Kierkegaard, *Fear and Trembling*, trans. Walter Lowrie (Princeton, 1952), p. 87.

98

Greeks; the godhead here appears as the power of social-human relationships." The gods in Greek tragedy are nothing more or less than the sphere of ethics; hence, Greek tragedy remains "the conflict of two ethical spheres; therefore, its whole substance is this-worldly" (II, 693). Marx's conclusion on the same question makes the point even more vividly: "If we consider the gods and heroes of Greek art without religious or aesthetic prejudices, we find in them nothing that could not exist in the pulsations of nature. Indeed, these images are artistic only as they portray beautiful human mores in a splendid integrated form."[5] Pursuing the contrast of Abraham and Agamemnon further, Lukács shows that the situation of the former remains mired in particularity, because the action is merely a private expression of faith unable to rise to any level of universal meaning. It is effective, at best, as an abstract paradigm. Thus, the Abraham-Isaac story is allegorical, while the Agamemnon-Iphigenia episode is symbolic-tragic, because the symbols make a genuine this-worldly, ethical conflict possible.

In broader terms, the judgment of Lukács is that when religion, theology, or any transcendental system of thought invades art, neither symbolism nor the art-work's "own world" is possible to achieve, because all particulars of the transcendental content must satisfy the exact prescriptions dogmatically attributed to them by systems outside art. Art must have freedom, not to separate itself from life, but to be capable, in both content and form, of "subtly adjusting itself to the concrete social needs of a constantly changing existence" (II, 696). If art resigns its right "to interpret independently" significant phenomena of social reality, including the interpretation of

[5] Mikhail Lifshitz, *The Philosophy of Art of Karl Marx* (New York, 1938), p. 26.

myths and legends, then it gives up any possibility for the development of new forms.

This great concern of Lukács with the problems and "emptiness" of allegory may seem a somewhat exaggerated anachronism to the reader, but when we recall his belief that modern literature is suffering from the invasion of allegory, we can understand the attention given it here. The apparently unparalleled revolution of new forms in modern literature is largely an illusion in the opinion of Lukács, because the innovations are only superficial, going only as deep as formalistic technique. In "modernism" the "world" is still contentless, seeking "aesthetic compensation in the decorative" (II, 718). The general relapse into allegory is real, although not simple. Old allegory made this-worldly reality shrink to near nothingness in favor of a transcendental, or heavenly, reality; it has in common with modern allegory the "destruction of direct sensuous reality" (II, 714). In place of a transcendental world prescribed by a specific church's dogmas, modern allegory tends to put forth a variety of related things, such as nothingness, anarchism, nihilism, and religious atheism. What all allegories have in common is that they lend themselves "par excellence to a description of man's alienation from objective reality."[6] Lukács recognizes that modern allegory also grows out of an essentially religious need, but this need takes the shape of a paradoxical religious atheism (e.g., Kafka, Beckett) showing "that the desire for salvation lives on with undiminished force in a world without God, worshipping the void created by God's absence."[7]

Lukács admits that the religious need, to which alle-

[6] Georg Lukács, *Realism in Our Time*, trans. John and Necke Mander (New York, 1964), p. 40.
[7] *Ibid.*, p. 44.

100

gorical, transcendental art responds, is a real and important fact of life. Therefore, while he considers the majority of such art (especially in the twentieth century) anti-human, destroying the dignity of man, he does not recommend a frontal attack upon either religion or "modernist" art, such as those which have been periodically attempted in the socialist countries. Optimistically, he perceives the solution to the problem in the larger context of the slow but successful accomplishment of the human-Promethean task of mankind, manifested from the *Genesis* where "man's transformation from half-animal being" is conceived as the work of Satan, through the Prometheus of Aeschylus, continuing with Dante's Satan, Milton's Lucifer "which explodes the theological outlines," young Goethe's Prometheus poems and *Faust*, through Dostoyevsky to Thomas Mann's *Faustus* novel, where "the satanic element is no more than an attempt to separate the destiny of the individual from that of mankind" (II, 772). With this, a humanist, enlightened, this-worldly focus is achieved, forming the basis for the destiny of all artistic practice. This art (along with science in its own manner) is capable of eliminating "the seemingly objectively given transcendent" (II, 774), an important factor in life only because the isolated individual can easily believe that he is surrounded by various transcendental elements. If (as in the case of the above-mentioned frontal attack) the feelings thus aroused in the individual, and the religious needs that are their bases, are not transformed into more productive, real "goals, authentic contents, greater intensities," through a humanist, this-worldly art able to unite the individual with mankind, then "the social and ideological defeat of the religious world view" can be only temporary (II, 758). This is also the problem, Lukács believes, with most

101

"modernist" writers for whom "unbelief has lost its revolutionary *élan*" but who were unable or unwilling to find any "meaning immanent in the world of the life of man," and, so, "the empty heavens" became for them "the projections of a world beyond hope of redemption."[8]

It is clear that in Lukács' analysis allegorical art is inseparably linked with a religious-transcendental world view, while symbolist art is the companion of a this-worldly (if not materialist) and humanist world view. Symbolism, in the Goethe-Lukács definition, is consistent with other important categories of Lukács' aesthetic theory (reflection, specialty, type, etc.) and the premises of his dialectical materialist philosophy. Lukács' acceptance of symbolism, carefully distinguished from allegory, as an organic part of the realistic art he advocates, enables him to defend his central reflection theory against attempts to attach the label of "naturalism" to it. The content of art is reproduction, he states, but the "reproduction of life's truth, which does not take into consideration even to the smallest degree, whether this truth is verifiable as the mirror-image of details" (ii, 779).

[8] *Ibid.*, pp. 40-44.

7.

FORM AND CONTENT IN ART

Much of Lukács' practical criticism, when dealing with the problems of form, gives the impression of de-emphasizing the importance of form in art. He often writes harshly of "empty formalism," of "decorative form" and form for its own sake—in other words, of any kind of overemphasis or predominance of artistic form. His theoretical writings, on the other hand, seem to give quite the opposite impression. He believes that artistic work is conscious, rational work, in which the forming of the art-work takes up the major share of the activity. His theories seem to suggest that form rather than content has the greater significance in art, because it has the final weight and is the element that comes into direct contact with the receiver. Yet these same writings often say clearly that content is of primary importance, because it is first in the sequence of artistic work and it determines the substance of the work. All of this may impress the reader that Lukács' attitude is wavering, indecisive, on the subject of form and content. But this is only seemingly so. The possible false impression is partly due to the fact that Lukács sometimes discusses, or comments upon, form and content separately. When all the comments are studied, a clear picture emerges, indicating that Lukács sees the relationship of form and content in artistic reflection as a dialectical one, the two completing one another in the individual work of art. In this sense they

103

are of equal importance, and the definition of one is impossible without the definition of the other.

In his most concise definition of this dialectical relationship, Lukács accepts Hegel's view of the subject in saying that content is none other than the "overflow" of form into content, while form is none other than the "overflow" of content into form.[1] This means that the selection of content is already artistic work. Form alone cannot lend something (just anything) beauty, and content (however carefully selected) does not constitute art if it is communicated to the receiver directly without the mediation of artistic form. Lukács believes that, prior to the artistic forming, the artist executes "preparatory" work, "aesthetic processing" on the raw content that is indispensable to and inseparable from artistic work, although in itself it is not yet as truly artistic work as "forming" is: "Forming is really the crucial factor, while the aesthetic processing of the content is merely preparatory work, which artistically means very little in itself, because staying with this brings about . . . aesthetically absolutely nothing. This lack of independence [of the preparation of content from forming] however, changes nothing in the primacy of content . . . such an artistic preparation of content is totally irreplaceable from the point of view of the creation of the final, truly artistic form."[2] So, while the final artistic value of a work is determined by the success of its form, achievement of it would be impossible without the artistic preparation of its content. In its final shape, then, the work of art rises out of life, but it does not radically break with life's con-

[1] György Lukács, *Az esztétikum sajátossága*, 1 (Budapest, 1969), p. 359.
[2] György Lukács, *A különösség, mint esztétikai kategória* (Budapest, 1957), p. 225.

104

tents, because the artistic preparation assures that they remain the foundation, the substance, of the work, thus maintaining its contact with objective reality. In this way it is entirely possible that a certain ethically extreme content of life become aesthetically effective (e.g., Richard III), if within the particular aesthetic "world" its relationship to that "world's" ethical standards is clearly established.[3] In other words, even the most detestable ethical content (action, character) can be a proper subject of art, if its treatment is not purely relativistic.

The task of defining form, then, must always include content as an organic part. Thus, artistic form is the "specific, peculiar form of that determined content, which is the content of the particular art-work."[4] Significantly, this implies that every individual art-work has its own peculiar form. It also implies that form does not (cannot) make something of nothing; it does not transform the abstract into concrete. But it can create "artistic reality from mere possibilities, it can perform qualitative changes on the direct, apparent structure of content."[5] Artistic form, in this way, can paradoxically become "unfaithful" to particular phenomena of objective reality. Thus, the consideration of totality (the "self-enclosed totality" of the art-work) is important, for it is achieved by means of form: "The art-work—with regard to its content—always gives only segments of reality. The task of artistic forming is to make sure that these do not have the effect of segments torn from totality, the comprehension and effectiveness of which would require us to relate it to its environment in space and time, rather that they have the effect of an enclosed whole which does not

---

[3] *Az esztétikum sajátossága*, II, p. 543.
[4] *A különösség, mint esztétikai kategória*, p. 151.
[5] *Ibid.*, p. 227.

require completion by means of external elements."[6] It
is generally recognized that one of the great achievements
of Gerhart Hauptmann's drama *The Weavers* is the excellent portrayal of the masses, the weavers, the collective
hero. When we analyze this specific achievement carefully, says Lukács, we find that Hauptmann used merely
ten to twelve weavers to achieve this convincing portrayal
of the masses.[7] The reason for the success is that the
weavers are selected and characterized in such a way,
placed in such situations, such interrelationships, that
from these forming principles the artistic impression of
the masses is created. In order to extend this example into
a general principle, Lukács states that "the entire content of the art-work must turn into form, if its true content is to bring about an aesthetic effect."[8]

The achievement of totality and, through it, aesthetic
effect, then, is one role of form in the general composition of the art-work. Another important role is the creation of type. One of the more serious problems in creating typical characters, for example, is the difficulty of
avoiding types as such. Lukács stresses that the typical
character must be fully sensuous, which can be accomplished only if form creates a unity between the individual and the type. This unity is not impartially created
because the characters, through their attitudes toward
life, either attract or dispel the receiver.[9] The individual
characters give the impression of independent life, and
to the extent that they are individuals they have independent lives, but their artistic existence (as types) has

[6] György Lukács, *Művészet és társadalom* (Budapest, 1968),
p. 128.
[7] *Ibid.*, p. 129.   [8] *Ibid.*, p. 130.
[9] *A különösség, mint esztétikai kategória*, p. 228.

106

a dynamic-mutual relationship with other artistic figures. In Sophocles' *Antigone*, for instance, Antigone could be characterized as an individual without her sister Ismene, but Ismene is indispensable to the characterization of Antigone as type. That does not mean, however, that more sisters or friends of Antigone could have made the portrayal of her type more complete. The character of Ismene is dramatically necessary "in order to show that Antigone's action is indeed a heroic and matter-of-course expression of an earlier morality that has already perished, but that in the present circumstances of the drama is no longer a spontaneously matter-of-course reaction."[10] The addition of a third sister, however, would have been pure tautology. Yet, without Ismene it would not have been clear whether the actions of Antigone are typical, eccentric, or average.

After he has established the relationship between form, totality, and type, the greatest source of difficulty for Lukács is coping with the "form-revolutions" of the twentieth century. He realizes that during the past several decades a number of radical changes have occurred in artistic form, exemplified by frequent "innovations," and that most of these have been ephemeral. He does not, however, attribute the rapidity of the changes to changes in fashions and tastes, believing that "behind every change in form, however unaware the 'revolutionaries' may be of this, there is a hidden change in the content of life."[11] Why, then, are the new forms so short-lived? First, they do not reach deeply into the real changes of life's content, reflecting certain new, but mere-

[10] Georg Lukács, *The Historical Novel*, trans. Hannah and Stanley Mitchell (London, 1962), p. 95.
[11] *A különösség, mint esztétikai kategória*, p. 192.

ly surface phenomena of life, catching "only a tiny corner, a little tip, a small splinter of the really new."[12] Second (a point that follows directly out of the first), since there is no search for depth in the "preparatory artistic work," all the energy is devoted to a nearly obsessive preoccupation with form alone. The result is that form as such becomes the main feature of most works of art. Lukács has always rejected the art of any period in which form is featured independently of content: "Every form, which enters the awareness of the receiver as form, because it preserves a degree of independence from content and does not overflow completely into the content, must necessarily create the effect that it is, to some extent, the expression of the poet's subjective being and not wholly a reflection of the object itself."[13] That expresses Lukács' summary of the problem of form in "modernism." He illustrates it through the comparison of the use of the "inner monologue" in two different contemporary novels. In one part of Thomas Mann's novel, *Lotte In Weimar*, the awakening Goethe "discusses" his situation, his relationship with Schiller, etc., in the form of an inner monologue. Looked at superficially, this resembles Mrs. Bloom's monologue in James Joyce's novel *Ulysses*. The difference is that in Mrs. Bloom's monologue Joyce wants only to express the fully "disorderly content" of what happens to come into the mind of such a woman, while in Mann's monologue, behind the facade of spontaneity, there hides a "carefully composed artistic-human summary."[14] The difference appears to be primarily in the contents of the two

[12] *Ibid.*

[13] *Művészet és társadalom*, p. 132.

[14] György Lukács, *Magyar irodalom—magyar kultúra* (Budapest, 1970), p. 615.

examples, but, according to Lukács, the final effect is that Joyce has only form to offer, while Mann offers form and content in a synthesis.

Content appearing independently of form may be of significant substance, therefore of great importance, but only as philosophical, ethical, political, etc., matter, not as art. Lukács believes that such contents (as in publicistic, propagandistic, naturalistic, etc., works), when claiming to be art, are just as subjective in nature as form appearing independently.[15] Only form can lend such contents aesthetic substance, aesthetic identity. Without artistic form such works are nothing more than the raw contents of sociological, political, etc., theories and, as such, they would be more effectively (certainly more objectively) communicated in scholarly essays and articles, or speeches. Lukács' sharp criticism of such works may not be as evident to the English-speaking reader as his criticism of so called "formalism," because too many of his works are untranslated. (Although he criticizes the works of Upton Sinclair along this line.[16]) Among his untranslated works, his writings on Hungarian literature,[17] especially the novel and the drama, contain much adverse criticism of "art" without artistic form.

It has already been established that in Lukács' aesthetic theory art is not only anthropomorphic but also anthropocentric. This means that the focal point, the central content of art, is man. We know also that when Lukács talks about man he tends to mean mankind, or the individual man as a member of humanity, society,

---

[15] *Művészet és társadalom*, p. 132.

[16] Georg Lukács, *Studies in European Realism* (New York, 1964), p. 257.

[17] *Magyar irodalom—magyar kultúra*, and *Népi irók a mérlegen* (Budapest, 1946).

109

community, etc., because he believes that man's individual existence cannot be distinguished from his social and historical environment. In general terms, then, the content of art is man as a social animal. In the individual artwork, whatever the direct starting point, goal, or concrete theme, it is content (the essential question: What is man?) that determines the form.[18] The formless, raw segment of life cannot evoke the aesthetic effect, or can do so only accidentally. Only the aesthetic form, as the mediating element, comes into direct contact with the receiver; only it can evoke the aesthetic effect. But if the form has "overflowed" into the content, if form and content are perfectly blended, integrated, if form is not perceivable as such (as it should be according to Lukács), then the receiver may be impressed with only the effect of the content: "The unity of content and form in aesthetics, the peculiar characteristic of artistic form that it is always the form of a special, individual content, is expressed . . . in the fact that the receiver is directly touched by the effects of the form, which, however, during the experience, instantly overflows into the content, and, therefore, the receiver believes that content affected him."[19] In the final analysis, then, the real basis, the fundamental determinant of the aesthetic effect, is the content of the art-work. This effect, however, would be impossible to achieve without the mediatory role of artistic form.

On the surface it seems that Lukács rejects the innumerable formalistic innovations of "modernist" literature for reasons of the extreme results of their experimentation with form. That is correct only to a certain extent. The fundamental reason for his rejection of much of

[18] *Művészet és társadalom*, p. 333.
[19] *Az esztétikum sajátossága*, I, p. 306.

"modernist" literature is the lack of content. He believes that a couple of lines from T. S. Eliot's poem "Wasteland" provide a fitting analogy to illustrate the content-lessness of "modernist" literature: "Shape without form, shade without color/ Paralyzed force, gesture without motion." Lukács does not reject any particular form as such; he rejects it only if it masquerades as a complete work of art. He finds it conceivable that any of those specific formalistic innovations might find their content and, thus, become aesthetically complete. The process, of course, would have to be reversed, because the "artistically prepared" content comes first, to which the appropriate form is sought.

Lukács insists that there is no art richer in new artistic form than realistic art, which satisfies the major principles of his reflection theory.[20] This conclusion follows logically if we accept Lukács' premises along the way: that is, that there is one objective reality that is constantly changing and developing, that art reflects this reality (this-worldliness) with man as a social animal at the center, and that this constantly changing content of art determines the form, each specific new content requiring a specifically new form. Nowhere can this be illustrated better than in the differences and similarities between Greek drama and Shakespearean drama. The outward and purely formal distinctions—such as large or small casts, simplicity or frequently changing colorful scenes, etc.—constitute a superficial and mistaken basis for pinpointing the basic differences.[21] (There can be dramatically superfluous characters even when there is outward simplicity, as in the case of the confidants in neo-classic tragedy.) The real differences result from the changes in

[20] *Az esztétikum sajátossága*, II, p. 780.
[21] *The Historical Novel*, p. 96.

content. Form changed because social reality (the basis of the content) had changed; therefore, the differences between the Greeks and Shakespeare is "an historical one."[22] The state of reality for Sophocles and Aeschylus was a simpler one than that of Shakespeare's age; therefore, Shakespeare invented "an entirely new and original system of social and human movements, typical and diverse,"[23] but his artistic method remained essentially the same as that of the Greeks, for he too achieved the creation of typical collisions and characters, reducing the diversity of his reality to what is typically necessary.

[22] *Ibid.*, p. 95.   [23] *Ibid.*

8.

THE AESTHETIC EFFECT

O NE impression that emerges clearly from Lukács' theory of aesthetic reflection is that he considers art a way of knowing. Art is not, however, simply an epistemological tool; its primary value is not social utility. He has said that art is man's "self-awareness" and "the memory of mankind," but those are much too abstract descriptions to satisfy. Only an examination of Lukács' theory of the prolonged and complex nature of the complete artistic experience can take one close to his meaning of the value of art. Such an examination reveals that Lukács considers pleasure to be an integral part of art, of the aesthetic effect: "It is not an exaggeration to say that art perhaps never would have come into being if pleasure were not an important, even vital, social constituent of the life of man. Man's habit of responding to certain phenomena of life positively or negatively within the outlines of pleasure is a crucial factor in the origin of every art."[1] Crucial though pleasure is, it is not the major factor in judging whether something is a work of art. Lukács would not altogether accept Lessing's statement that "the only unpardonable fault of a tragic poet is this, that he leaves us cold,"[2] which clearly implies the dominating

[1] György Lukács, *Az esztétikum sajátossága*, II (Budapest, 1969), p. 516. Further references to this work in this chapter will be identified parenthetically (by volume and page) in the text.

[2] G. E. Lessing, *Hamburg Dramaturgy*, trans. Helen Zimmern (New York, 1962), p. 45.

113

importance of pleasure (emotion) as a criterion for judging a tragedy. Although Lukács accepts Plotinus' contribution in moving away from Plato's categorical rejection of pleasure (II, 491), the "ecstasy" principle of Longinus or the "intoxication" theory of Nietzsche are far too extreme for him. He points out that in reflection both content and form are capable of arousing pleasure without being part of a genuine work of art. He cites, on the one hand, detective novels and crime films, whose contents give pleasure to certain segments of society and, on the other, such truly great works in form as the plays of Beckett, whose formalistic achievements are greater than those of many "deep and true art-works" and so arouse pleasure, that are not art in the final analysis. Lukács states emphatically that "we must seek and find the final determining criterion of genuine art in its universality" (II, 516). One might argue that the works of Beckett are certainly universal, but to Lukács their universality is expressed too abstractly and allegorically. Universality in art, for Lukács, is arrived at only through the category of specialty, through the observation of the principles of type, totality, and this-worldliness.

Before describing the components of his theory of the aesthetic effect, Lukács makes it clear that he rejects both illusion and empathy as being important or unique parts of that effect. He contends that illusion, as a goal of the aesthetic effect, is basically a deception, cheating, which places art on the level of daydreams, because "illusion is merely subjective" and "starting from this subjectivity it wants to correct objective reality, that is, it wants to replace it with a better reality woven from subjective dreams" (I, 767). Lukács believes that we, the receivers of the art-work, are always aware of the difference be-

114

tween objective reality and the aesthetic world. He considers the suggestion that the receiver might knowingly surrender himself to illusion degrading to art. The only anthropomorphic reflection that is based on illusion is religion, because religion demands absolute belief. Empathy is not at all unique to art, for it is a common occurrence in everyday life. To make empathy the core of artistic experience means to drag artistic experience down to the level of everyday life. Moreover, an extreme form of empathic response is the Nietzschean "Dionysiac intoxication" that Lukács opposes very sharply with the following argument: "This intoxication is the desperate gesticulation of those men who cannot find direction and content for their lives. The transcendence, which they believe they grasp in it, is the Nothingness of their own shattered and crippled personalities, the emptiness of their relationship with the world. When with feigned pride they refuse to embrace the world with the help of science and mimesis, they are merely deluding themselves . . . but when they plunge back from the intoxication into everyday life, which now seems even emptier, the world still regains its rightful status" (1, 481). Whether it is the Hitlers or drugs that cause these short excursions of people into "transcendence," Lukács believes they invariably have to come back to facing the facts of objective reality. He does not believe that theories of transcendence are verifiable on the basis of the best artistic accomplishments of mankind. If the essence of artistic experience were such "intoxications," then art would be as dehumanizing as the effects of drug addiction and alcoholism.

Perhaps the clearest way to discuss Lukács' theory of the complete artistic experience is by way of stating first

115

that he considers the ultimate effect of art to be ethical in nature. By this he does not mean that art seeks to interfere with the practical lives of men, that it serves out sermons, moral codes, or object lessons. He is talking about a long, subtle, uneven process (emotional and rational) that occurs in the receiver after the aesthetic effect proper. Collectively, this is a socio-historical effect of awakening man's consciousness to the fact that he "makes himself" and to the broadening of the concept of the individual man as a member of ongoing humanity. The final effect, in Lukács' judgment, appears to fall somewhere between "disinterested contemplation" and direct, practical influence: "There is a deep relationship between aesthetics and ethics, revealing the fact that a truly profound aesthetic development is not possible without regard to moral problems and feelings; in the realm of aesthetics, however, these feelings must remain contemplative (only after the aesthetic experience can they assume the form of moral practice), therefore, the problems remain problems, they 'merely' broaden man's horizon and reveal conditions and consequences otherwise doomed to oblivion, without going over into practice in a direct manner" (1, 487-88). Keats summarized the final effect of art with the line: "Beauty is truth, truth beauty." Lukács finds this poetic expression of the complete union of ethics and aesthetics totally acceptable: "The identity of Beauty and Truth is indeed the direct meaning of the pure aesthetic experience, and this is why it is the eternal theme of all theories about art" (1, 489).

The total artistic experience that results in this ultimately ethical effect consists of three parts: (1) the receiver's inner state before the effect, (2) the aesthetic effect (catharsis) itself, and (3) the after-effect. The "before" of the effect is extremely important because

116

"the receiver never faces the art-work as tabula rasa";[3] rather he "comes from life, more or less loaded with impressions, experiences and ideas" (I, 749), all of which continue to play an important role both in the catharsis and the after-effect. Every receiver comes to the work as a "whole man of life," an individual with his personal worries, goals, and desires, but only journalistic, rhetorical, or propagandistic works, whose contents (without aesthetic transformation through form) remain the contents of everyday life, are directed at man in such inner state of being, because only such works aim "to ease directly the implementation of definite, concrete social tasks" (I, 751). Lukács cites Aeschylus' *The Persians*, the plays of Aristophanes, Brieux, and the early plays of Brecht as examples of rhetorical drama directed at the receiver as a "whole man of everyday life." A true art-work's content, on the other hand, through its peculiar form (its "own world"), breaks into the "whole man's" soul-complex transforming his inner state of being and causing him to "suspend his other concrete endeavors and to give himself solely to the effect of the art-work" (I, 749). This experience changes him temporarily from an isolated individual with individual concerns to a participant in "man's wholeness" whose concern is the destiny of humanity.

The core of the aesthetic effect itself is catharsis or the purging of passions. Lukács is careful to make the reservation, however, that the aesthetic effect is not purely emotional. He shares Brecht's skepticism about all "merely emotional artistic effects," while insisting, as he believes Brecht also does, on the preservation of the "seed of catharsis" (I, 765). Lukács argues that events in real life,

[3] György Lukács, *Művészet és társadalom* (Budapest, 1968), p. 326.

even scientific revelations (such as those of Copernicus or Darwin), are capable of arousing strong emotions in nearly every member of society due to their religious, political, scientific, etc., implications; therefore, the achievement of heightened emotion is not in itself unique to art. Nor is catharsis comparable to the calm after the storm or quiet resignation; in fact it has no negative or pessimistic connotations at all. Lukács quite clearly favors Lessing's definition of catharsis as "the transformation of passions into virtuous habits,"[4] but he broadens the presence of catharsis to include the effects of every single art. The emotional effect, the purging of the passions in all arts, has, in his optimistic view, a broadly humanizing influence upon the receiver: "That moving and shaking effect, that convulsion which is provided by tragedy, comedy, the novel, the good painting, the good statue and the musical creation, that purging of our passions, causes us to become better human beings than we were, to develop in us the readiness for the morally good."[5] Catharsis in art "evokes that moving experience which reveals how different, how new—at once more individual, more comprehensive, more universal—reality can be."[6] Since the center of art is man, Lukács' concept of catharsis recalls Sophocles' words in *Antigone*, "The world is full of wonderful things/ But none more so than man," and Shakespeare's "What a piece of work is man" (*Hamlet*, II, ii). There is a definite sense of joy in the experience. The aesthetic effect changes the "whole man of everyday life" into one with a sense of "man's wholeness" by "forcing onto him a new 'world,' " by filling him

[4] Lessing, *Hamburg Dramaturgy*, p. 193.

[5] György Lukács, "A müvészet mint felépitmény" (a special publication of the Hungarian Cultural Ministry, 1955), p. 26.

[6] György Lukács, *Utam Marxhoz*, II (Budapest, 1971), p. 508.

with "new or freshly seen contents," and by making him capable of taking in this "world" with "rejuvenated senses and thinking" (I, 748).

The consideration of the collision of the new and the old is very important to Lukács. During the artistic experience, he believes, there is frequently a battle in the receiver between his old experiences and the present artistic impressions. The effect of great art is precisely its capacity to make "the new, the original" victorious over the old experiences of the receiver.[7] The deeply moving, even shaking, emotional-aesthetic experience is necessary because only the most extreme trials can prove the individual's true being, "whether he is seed or peeling." Nothing exemplifies this more poignantly than Ibsen's *Peer Gynt*. At the end of a series of extreme trials Peer sits peeling an onion layer by layer only to discover that it has no "heart," no seed, no substance (v, v). This symbolic summary of the tragic character's life illustrates what Lukács means by art's, especially drama's, probing for man's "intensive totality." Aesthetic experiences of extreme intensity can best evoke "the purging of passions" and the consequent "overflow into ethics" in the "after" stage of the aesthetic effect (II, 368). It is for this reason that "tragedy brings about the most succinct, most characteristic form of catharsis" (I, 760).

Whatever else may be the value of an artistic work for man, its ultimate aesthetic value is its potential power to bring about this cathartic experience for the receiver in any succeeding age. Lukács illustrates this quite clearly through some comments on the *Oedipus Rex* of Sophocles: "It is true that the *Oedipus* of Sophocles is loaded with information valuable to the ancient historian. But it is equally true that nine-tenths of the later

[7] *Művészet és társadalom*, p. 326.

viewers or readers of this drama know nothing or very little about such historical preconditions, and yet, they are still deeply moved by its effect. It would be, however, another false extreme to believe that this effect is due exclusively to the 'magic' of the perfect form. The perfect form is there . . . but by itself it is empty and would arouse only a short-lived effect of suspense. . . . What moves the listener in the *Oedipus* is a typical human destiny, in which today's man, too—living through it—even if he is only capable of understanding the concrete historical conditions in their crudest outlines, awakens directly-emotionally to the awareness of a *mea causa agitur*."[8] The reason for the long-lasting life, the unceasing evocative power, of all such dramas lies in this effect. They awaken man's own past, but not the personal past of the particular individual, rather "his past as a member of mankind."[9]

The transformation of "the whole man of everyday life" into man's sense of wholeness as a member of ongoing humanity resulting from the aesthetic (cathartic) effect is temporary. "After" the experience the receiver goes back to his personal goals, problems, and desires. What influence the art-work has had upon him is difficult to measure, because the effect varies from individual to individual and is likely to be cumulative: "The effect of the art-work upon man after the experience remains almost completely imperceptible, and only a whole series of similar experiences will reveal visible attitudinal, cultural, etc., changes; frequently, of course, a single artwork may bring a complete turnabout in a man's life" (1, 785). For the most part the individual man's interests

[8] *Ibid.*, p. 324.
[9] György Lukács, A *különösség, mint esztétikai kategória* (Budapest, 1957), p. 239.

change very slowly and subtly as the result of the aesthetic effect. Lukács adds that any change in the interests of the receiver is "only a possibility" and by no means a necessity. Further, whatever the size, the quality, or the speed of the change may be, the change itself is "not the criterion of either the power of the art-work, or the depth of the catharsis" (ii, 489). When the aesthetic effect does influence individual interests it is indirectly done, because the cathartic effect directly touches only man's sense of wholeness and modifies individual interests only through it.

Lukács is careful to note that this does not mean that his theory is close to Kant or the advocates of "art for art's sake," who believe "that artistic experiences do not influence people's practical, everyday lives" (i, 775). Disinterestedness, according to Lukács, is only one factor and not the essence of the aesthetic attitude. Participants in the artistic experience suspend their direct practical goals only temporarily. Total disinterestedness is not possible because the mere fact that the receiver "embraces," takes in, the art-object is "inseparably linked with his affirmation or negation of it" (i, 606). The opposite extreme—that art is didactic and artists are "engineers of the soul" (as Stalin put it)—is even further from Lukács. He rejects Brecht's theories, because he believes Brecht wants art to achieve "during" the experience what Lukács says can occur only in the "after" stage of the aesthetic effect. (Still, Lukács finds Brecht's late plays "aesthetically significant art-works," born despite Brecht's theories, which shove aside all hitherto existing theories.) What Lukács concludes, then, is that the aesthetic effect does influence the receiver's practical goals and desires, but that the effect is not aimed at this directly and the influence is not immediate. The aesthetic effect does not solve any of the receiver's problems, complex or simple, personal or social, but it does "develop a human readiness." To translate this readiness into practical actions, the receiver must find the necessary tools in life itself. The real power of artistic evocation is that it enlarges the receiver's picture about himself and the world in which he lives. Thus, in the total aesthetic experience there is no complete separation between life and art. In Lukács' metaphor, "life is a great river" from which the reflective forms of a higher order (art, science, philosophy, etc.) branch off, achieve their own peculiar forms and "join once again the river of everyday life by virtue of their influence upon the lives of men" (1, 9). As a result of this unending historical process, both life and art are constantly enriched.

The fact that Lukács finds the ultimate effect of all arts to be ethical, that he accepts the thesis that truth and beauty are identical, does not mean that he wishes to impose external ethical standards on art. He has always rejected the critical methods of Plato and all other extrinsic criticism, agreeing instead with Aristotle's intrinsic approach: "Aristotle has also said that the artistic pleasure, the beautiful experience that occurs in the reception of the object, has nothing to do with whether we would welcome its (man, situation, event, etc.) coming to fruition as concrete reality of our lives. The essence of the aesthetic creation and its effect is that in the artistic portrayal man embraces without resistance, even enthusiastically, all that he fears, abhors, or rejects in life" (1, 642). Lukács is not a dualist; he spurns all theories that attempt to build a hierarchic ordering of natural and artistic beauty. Natural beauty is an element of life that, like all other elements of life, is a form and content outside the realm of aesthetics. The artist does not create artistic beauty by merely transferring the beautiful from life into the art-work. He creates aesthetic beauty by making the elements of life integral parts of the total context of the art-work's own world. In this sense, natural ugliness as well as natural beauty can be aesthetically beautiful. But in a true work of art it is not perceived as natural ugliness, because art is not judged by the standards of everyday life.

Even in lyric poetry, which often seems to be merely the celebration of the beauty of nature, Lukács believes that "the poetic formulation of spring or winter also betrays the position that the poet takes with regard to the truly great currents and battles of his age" (II, 595). Art is anthropomorphic; everything in it is related to man. In the novel and the drama this is even clearer: "The subject of these is not the mere experiencing of reality . . . rather the human or social practice itself; the experiencing of nature becomes the proper subject of structuring only episodically, tightly related to this practice" (II, 595). Lukács gives many examples of the occurrence of natural beauty in art in this fashion, citing especially Greek and Elizabethan drama. He stresses that it would be as much a mistake to say that the Greeks found storms at sea beautiful simply because such storms are often parts of aesthetically beautiful, whole art-works, as to conclude that the storm in *King Lear* is not primarily music accompanying a human story "whose guiding motifs are given by the social-ethical problems" (II, 596).

Beauty in art is the portrayal of the totality of man. In true art this is not done in a roundabout manner: not, for example, by arousing pity and sympathy through elegiacally lamenting the past and the dying, or taking revenge for its destruction by means of poetic irony—as Schiller had predicted, and Lukács believes has indeed

123

occurred, in modern bourgeois literature. The ultimate effect of the art-work should point to the future. Its beauty lies in its ability to rescue man from the distorting and destructive effects of class society through the "poetically direct portrayal of man's wholeness."[10]

[10] György Lukács, *Nagy orosz realisták, kritikai realizmus* (Budapest, 1951), p. 47.

9.

THE UNIQUE PRINCIPLES
OF DRAMA

THE fundamental principles of Lukács' aesthetic theory so far discussed—realistic reflection, special category, type, totality, symbolism, and the aesthetic effect—apply to all arts. They are, as we have seen, not rigid prescriptions, mechanical rules invented by theorists and scholars, but, rather, flexible principles that have evolved through the many centuries, constantly enriched, clarified, defined, renewed, and broadened by each new individual work of art, because each new work finds its own specific, peculiar artistic form rooted in its dialectical relationship with its specific content. Beyond these generally applicable aesthetic principles, Lukács, in his work *The Peculiarity of Aesthetics*, discusses all specific art-forms at some length. Even architecture, gardening, and the art of film receive considerable treatment. But, throughout Lukács' writing career, the art of literature receives the greatest amount of attention both in theory and practical criticism. Within literature, the epic is treated most extensively, followed closely by the drama. The subject of the present chapter, following as it does the discussion of the significant general aesthetic principles of Lukács, is the examination of those important principles which Lukács considers uniquely characteristic of the art of drama. For the most part, comedy is not included in the discussion, because Lukács says very little about the subject, concentrating instead on tragedy.

Lukács' first task is to differentiate between the major literary forms: the epic (or novel), the drama, and lyric poetry. The basis for this is contained in his theory of reflection, which is built upon his materialistic, this-worldly philosophical world view: "Both tragedy and great epic—epic and novel—present the objective, *outer* world; they present the inner life of man only insofar as his feelings and thought manifest themselves in deeds and actions, in a visible interaction with objective, outer reality. This is the decisive dividing line between epic and drama, on the one hand, and lyric, on the other. Further, great epic and drama both give a *total picture* of objective reality."[1] While both the novel and the drama portray the totality of the life-process, Lukács, following Hegel, finds the core of the differences between the two in that the novel is characterized by the "totality of objects," and the drama by the "totality of movement."[2] Lukács further agrees with Hegel's statement that the "conflict of opposing elements" in life "is peculiarly adapted to the subject-matter of dramatic art,"[3] when he declares that the essential, dynamic center of this "totality of movement" is the dramatic collision. Drama is in a sense more skeletal, more saturated, more concentrated than is the novel, the backbone of the concentration being the central conflict. In drama there is no room for any psychological or moral tautology. One key factor in the nature of the collision or conflict in drama is that it is in the form of dramatic generalization. (In his discussion

[1] Georg Lukács, *The Historical Novel*, trans. Hannah and Stanley Mitchell (London, 1962), p. 90.

[2] *Ibid.*, p. 93.

[3] G.W.F. Hegel, *The Philosophy of Fine Art*, I, trans. F.P.B. Osmaston (London, 1920), p. 273.

of the special category Lukács has shown that drama is closer to the general, universal category than the novel.)

Illustrating this point through the example of *King Lear*, Lukács shows that in this play Shakespeare "embodies the older generation of the family only through Lear and Gloucester."[4] What in a novel would be necessary—to show the total life-circumstances of both the parents and the children—would amount to superfluous material here. The concentration in the reflection of the totality of life here is accomplished by grouping all manifestations of life around a great collision. The extreme and "typical movements" are, in this way, concentrated in a closed system, "the dialectics of which exhaust all the possible human attitudes to the collision."[5] Thus, instead of a totality of objects, of details, the result is a drama with its material reduced to the essential and the typical: "The portrayal is reduced to the typical representation of the most important and most characteristic attitudes of men, to what is indispensable to the dramatic working-out of the collision, to those social, human and moral *movements* in men, therefore, out of which the collision arises and which the collision dissolves."[6] Lukács believes that Shakespeare's plays (despite their outward appearance to the contrary because of large casts and double plots), as well as those of the Greek dramatists, always satisfy this principle of reduction to the typical dramatic representation. On the other hand, neo-classic dramas (with their superfluous confidants and mechanical collisions) or naturalistic dramas (such as Hauptmann's *The Weavers*, which include characters "to illustrate the social *milieu*," thus expressing the totality of

---

[4] *The Historical Novel*, p. 94. [5] *Ibid.*, pp. 93-94.
[6] *Ibid.*, p. 94.

objects) contain many elements alien in nature to the aim of drama. Admitting that what he described as "reduction to typical" is, to some extent, the distancing from life of the dramatic form, Lukács nevertheless insists that in reality it is no more than "a heightened and concentrated expression of certain tendencies of life itself."[7]

The laws of drama are the laws of actual life, the particular plays being "artistic images" of these laws. The principles of artistic reflection remain in effect and "the drama is a true work of art, if these are applied and observed."[8] More specifically, it is the collision, the core material of drama, that arises directly out of life. Lukács asserts that there are certain typical and significant collisions in life that are suitable to dramatic treatment. He calls these manifestations "facts of life tending toward drama," and, without denying the possibility of others, discusses five such "facts of life" as most significant.[9] Number one is the category of collisions portraying great historical revolutions. Lukács believes that the greatest tragedies of the history of drama arose out of periods when the most momentous world-historical changes were taking place in society. He cites Greek and Elizabethan dramas as the most superb examples and makes it clear that this category is by no means limited to violent revolutions. The reference here is rather to those long periods, sometimes encompassing centuries, during which one form of society goes through a transformation (development) into another more advanced form. Dramas reflecting such world-historical transformations, of course, portray the collisions of social forces only "at their most extreme and acute points."

[7] *Ibid.*, p. 105.　　[8] *Ibid.*　　[9] *Ibid.*, pp. 96-103.

The second type of collision consists of the portrayal of contradictions in life, in society, which are subtle, complicated, and do not alone result in world-historical changes. This is dramatic material if the principle of "typical collision" is observed and the portrayal is not overly localized. The "parting-of-the-ways in the lives of individuals and of society," as exemplified by the king's crucial decision in Hebbel's *Herod and Mariamne*, illustrates this kind of drama. In disagreement with those who advocate "drama without conflict" in socialist societies, Lukács adds that the "contradictoriness of life" lives on even in socialism, because the problems, struggle, hence conflict, continue to exist. Only the antagonistic nature of the conflicts is eliminated in socialism.

Lukács calls the dramas built upon the third type of collision on his list "day of reckoning" dramas. This kind of drama is constructed on the foundation of "that dramatic movement in life itself, in which the accumulation of consequences is transformed into action." Sophocles' *Oedipus Rex* and Büchner's *Danton's Death* exemplify this drama of individuals who, as a result of earlier actions, come to a point in life where they must settle their accounts. The collision springing from this kind of situation is considered by Lukács one of the central problems of drama.

The fourth type of collision, again found in life, is rooted in the "human response at certain turning-points in life." In G. B. Shaw's comedy *The Devil's Disciple*, as a result of seemingly unconscious choices, both Richard Dudgeon and Pastor Anderson make startling discoveries about themselves. Although these are extreme cases, Lukács believes that they illustrate how a character's choice, made from a number of possibilities, can put

129

his entire life on new foundations.[10] Finally, the deep involvement of a person in his work often produces significant collisions. Lukács emphasizes that such a case is dramatic material only if the nature of the individual's work and his involvement in it is not simply a matter of concern to himself. Brecht's *Galileo* comes to mind as an illustration. The common denominator of all of these collisions, and others that might exist, is that they are to be found in life. Lukács does not believe that a dramatist can concoct forms of collisions that do not already exist in society. The true dramatic genius selects a form of collision from the material of life and events only within the boundaries imposed by the nature of that collision.

Since Lukács puts primary emphasis on the conflict in drama, it follows that he considers dramatic characterizations of central importance. In an essay written in 1908, before his acquaintance with the ideas of Hegel, he already talks about drama as the "poetry of the will."[11] Later writings recognize the necessary interrelatedness of character and conflict, that "the convergence of character and collision is the fundamental basis of drama." The characters represent the clashing forces through their personal passions, which form the material basis of the conflict. Only typical-symbolic characters can fulfill this task, characters in whom, beyond their individuality, "the characteristic factors of the time have been thoroughly and organically assimilated" to the point where they have become "factors in their personal behavior."[12] If the characters and the conflict are to be "organically assimilated," and if the conflict is not invented but found in life, it follows logically that the characters themselves must also

[10] György Lukács, *Művészet és társadalom* (Budapest, 1968), p. 336.
[11] *Ibid.*, p. 20.   [12] *The Historical Novel*, p. 118.

130

be found in life. Indeed, Lukács, in agreement with Hegel, is of the opinion that the "world-historical individual" is best as the central figure of drama.

The "world-historical individual" is not be understood as only that historically authentic and important leader whose personal conflicts and decisions directly decide the destiny of nations. Even bourgeois characters—such as those in Lessing's *Emilia Galotti*, Schiller's *Intrigue and Love*, or Ostrovsky's *The Thunderstorm*—can be "world-historical individuals" if, as in these plays, "the inner social substance of the collision" manifested through the characters makes an historically and socially decisive event of the action of the drama. Poetic truth should not be sacrificed for the sake of faithfulness to historical facts in the characterization of such individuals. The really important elements that characterize the "world-historical individual" are a combination of "individual passion" and "social substance." It is for these reasons that Lukács dismisses as unimportant Hegel's criticism of Shakespeare's "inauthentic" characterization of Macbeth. The guiding principle that allows the creation of fruitful dramatic works does not consist in the externals, but in the "inner connection" between the characters at the "centre of the drama and the concrete collision of the social-historical forces."[13] The material for the characterization of such individuals is not so much to be invented, or to be found in the pages of history books, as to be discovered in life itself: "The greatness of *dramatic characterization*, the ability to make characters *live dramatically* does not only depend, therefore, on the playwright's ability to create character in itself, but rather, indeed above all, upon how far it is given him, subjectively and objectively, to discover the characters and collisions in

[13] *Ibid.*, p. 114.

131

reality that will correspond to these inner requirements of dramatic form."[14] If both the "individual passion" and the "social substance" are present in the play, but are not organically combined in the major characters, there is still a serious deficiency. For example, while in *Romeo and Juliet* the "subjectivity of the passion" of the lovers and "the universality of the collision" are seen by Lukács to form an organic unity, he believes that Ford's *'Tis Pity She's a Whore* falls short of this: "The love of the brother and sister is too eccentric, too subjective to be able to carry a dramatic action. The action takes refuge in the heroes' souls, whose passion is thus opposed, dramatically, merely by a prohibition in general, thus something quite foreign and abstract in relation to the passion."[15] By this Lukács does not mean to suggest that the individualization of the principal heroes of drama is not crucially important. He is saying, rather, that extremely subjective characterization, as well as overemphasis of the externals (e.g., historical facts) can destroy the typicalness, the relative universality, of the conflict.

The problems of what Lukács calls "fetishism" and "overmotivation" in characterization are closely related to the above-described issues. The influence of "fetishism" consists of the exaggerated external descriptions, whether in the author's stage directions or his narrative (as in the novel), which treat characters as things. Lukács reminds us that the drama, with the exception of the last century or so, never described its characters, yet they remained as lively impressions in the consciousness of humanity for many centuries. On the other hand, "the nineteenth century raised the sensual external literary portrayal to a particularly high point" in both the novel

[14] *Ibid.*   [15] *Ibid.*, p. 113.

and the drama; yet, to take an extreme example, none of Zola's characters (with the possible exception of Nana), lives particularly vividly in our memories today.[16] Lukács adds that elements in a dramatic work, such as external descriptions, which are unnecessary from the point of view of that art-work, are not only superfluous but also burdensome and confusing.

Beyond and deeper than the problems arising out of exaggerated character description, Lukács views the question of "overmotivation" as even more significant. His position on Hegel's objection to Shakespeare's exclusion from *Macbeth* of the title character's right to the throne as a motivation for his actions has already been referred to. Lukács sees these remarks of Hegel as one of the first examples of the increasing demands for overmotivation which began in the nineteenth century. The result of these demands was that "literature became burdened with overly defined (and poetically superfluous) justifications, which divested the composition of the whole and the parts of its slenderness without making the poetic content any more weighty."[17] A successful example of this poetic "slenderness" is this: "Romeo glances at Juliet—and the tragedy begins."[18] It occurs to no one to ask: Why did he fall in love with her and not someone else? On the other hand, the lack of poetic "slenderness" is obvious in the dramas of Strindberg, particularly *Miss Julie*, where the author incorporates an almost unending list of motives into the characterization of Miss Julie. In even more vivid contrast to the example of *Romeo and Juliet* is Hebbel's *Agnes Bernauer*, in which the author "wastes an entire act to offer reasons for the irresistible

[16] György Lukács, *Az esztétikum sajátossága*, 1 (Budapest, 1969), p. 671.
[17] *Ibid.*, p. 673.   [18] *Ibid.*

beauty of the heroine," although, from the dramatic point of view, the mere fact of Albert's falling in love with her would have been enough.[19] In short, Lukács favors the examples of the Greek and Shakespearean plays, in which, despite their apparent differences, the dramatic characterizations are simple, poetically "slender," and always lucid.

Lukács observes that in the historical novel the great figures of history are minor characters. On the other hand, "drama, by its very nature, demands for them the central role." Does this mean that, after all, the major characters of the drama must be real historical figures of importance? No, says Lukács, it only means that while in the novel the major characters tend to be at the periphery of great collisions, in drama, because it "concentrates on the decisive moments of a social-historical crisis," the major characters often are great historical figures.[20] It should be added that Lukács does not believe that only great historical conflicts are proper material for the drama. In fact, many dramatically portrayed conflicts, though unrecorded in history, bear a more significant historical character than numerous well-known historical events: "The greatest historical occurrence may appear thoroughly empty and unreal in drama, while less important events . . . can evoke the impression of the downfall of an epoch or the birth of a new world. It is enough to think of the great tragedies of Shakespeare, *Hamlet* or *Lear*, to see clearly how much a personal destiny can evoke the impression of a great historical change."[21] Nevertheless, whether the event of the drama is historically real or unreal on the face, the central con-

[19] *Ibid.*
[20] *The Historical Novel*, pp. 125-26.
[21] *Ibid.*, p. 118.

flict is from life itself. If the event is historically real, the dramatist's major obligation is still not to portray authentically the specific event or the historical figures involved in it, but to give an authentic portrayal of the essence of the conflict itself.

In dealing with the concept of necessity and the accidental elements in drama, Lukács takes the position that the internal causal relationship of the scenes is not the sole determinant of necessity. It is not at all satisfactory simply to divide the world up into two dualistically rigid categories: the necessary and the accidental. The correct criterion must be to perceive the hazy territory, the infinite number of "steps and transitions," in the relationship of these elements.[22] Using merely the cause-effect chain as the guilding principle would result in the rejection of several scenes (as unnecessary) in both *Hamlet* and *King Lear*. Lukács maintains that parallel and contrasting elements, so frequently used by Shakespeare, are justifiable as "necessary" artistic means for deepening the dimensions of the essential substance (e.g., character), and not merely because they happen to fit the cause-effect necessity pattern. Dramatic necessity remains "the supreme persuasive force of drama," but what specifically will be judged as necessary in a particular play is determined by the content, "the essential substance," the "central question," by the "inner . . . accord between the character (with his dominant passion which evokes the drama) and the social-historical essence of the collision."[23] If the elements of this connection are present, "then every individual accident, as at the close of *Romeo and Juliet*, occurs in an *atmosphere of necessity*, and in and through this atmosphere its accidental char-

[22] *Az esztétikum sajátossága*, I, p. 708.
[23] *The Historical Novel*, p. 121.

acter is dramatically erased."[24] A more serious violation of the principle of dramatic necessity occurs when the playwright's subjective intentions, his prejudices, interfere with the logical sequence of the action. Such "arbitrary" arrangement of scenes is among the flaws of *The Tragedy of Man*, written by the nineteenth-century Hungarian dramatist Imre Madách. According to Lukács, this play is an excellent example of a drama in which what happens in several particular scenes is necessitated not by the inner force of the character and situation but by the author's compelling desire to illustrate his thesis.[25]

Lukács also rejects the nineteenth-century bourgeois concept of fatalism as an element of dramatic necessity. He believes that the real issues contained in that view—the fight of the new and the old, the class struggle, and the philosophers' defense of the social status quo—are hidden behind the veil of justification in the name of cosmic laws: "The issue is the 'rightfulness' of the existing (feudal, absolutistic) system, whether every revolutionary which opposes the 'existing' system indeed commits a 'tragic' crime and, therefore, rightfully, necessarily meets his destruction; of course, his destruction then brings about certain changes in the existing system: liberal reforms. In other words, the Hegelians' theory of tragedy, with its 'necessity,' 'sin,' etc., is intended, on the one hand, to justify every monstrosity of class-society as cosmically necessary, . . . on the other hand, it endeavors to prove the futility of every revolutionary movement."[26] The abstract pessimistic world view that grows out of this concept of fatalism meets with equally strong rejection

[24] *Ibid.*
[25] György Lukács, *Magyar irodalom—magyar kultúra* (Budapest, 1970), p. 572.
[26] *Művészet és társadalom*, p. 291.

from Lukács. Bourgeois aesthetics (Schopenhauer, Nietzsche, Hebbel, Wagner), which linked together inseparably tragedy and the pessimistic world view, are categorically opposed by him: "The greatest tragedies of our heritage did not at all portray the necessary futility and condemnation of human endeavor. On the contrary, they portrayed the always concrete and forever returning fight of the old and the new, in which the crumbling of the old, or the defeat by the old of the still weak and undeveloped new, is crowned by the coming into reality of a higher order of development, or at least the perspective of such development."[27] He lists Aeschylus' *Prometheus Bound* and *The Oresteia* and Shakespeare's *Macbeth*, *King Lear*, and *Richard III* as examples in support of this contention.

One may conclude without exaggeration that Lukács' theory of tragedy is optimistic, which sets him at opposite poles from the theory of Schopenhauer. Responsible for this theory of tragedy is Lukács' historical view of life. He admits it is frequently true that for an individual there is no solution to life's conflicts. But from a broader, historical point of view there is no conflict without solution and, in the long run, perhaps no insurmountable obstacle. In any case, the futility of an individual's struggle is not the futility of life in general. In fact, just the opposite is true: "Every really great drama expresses, amid the horror of the necessary downfall of the best representatives of human society, amid the apparently inescapable, mutual destruction of men, an *affirmation of life*. It is a *glorification of human greatness*. Man, in his struggle with the objectively stronger forces of the social external world, in the extreme exertion of all his powers in this unequal battle, reveals important qualities

[27] *Ibid.*, p. 298.

which would otherwise have remained hidden. The collision raises the dramatic hero to a new height, the possibility of which he did not suspect in himself before. The realization of this possibility produces the enthusing and uplifting qualities of drama."[28] On the basis of these principles, Lukács salvages Sophocles' *Oedipus Rex* from the category of dramas of destiny. It is rather a "day of reckoning" drama, because the road that leads to the discovery is paved with the untiring initiative of Oedipus himself.

Individual initiative is a factor of primary importance in drama. Both drama and the novel, in order to bring a faithful image of life, should "reflect correctly the dialectics of freedom and necessity." Both should present the actions of man as "bound by the circumstances of his activity, by the social historical basis of his deeds."[29] But, while in the novel, which reflects the "totality of objects," the "circumstances" play a large role, in drama the relevant circumstances are given only in broad outlines, with the individual initiative taking the foreground. The factors of fate, "biological determinants," and the environment are, therefore, of considerably smaller significance in drama than the characterizations that shape the faithful portrayals of the collisions of human life.

Although Lukács believes that the drama has autonomous aesthetic existence independently of its performance in the theatre,[30] for its fullest impact the dramatic conflict must be experienced by spectators. In other words, the final analysis reveals that drama is public in character, making its impact upon the "publicly assembled multitude"; therefore, "it must possess a great deal

[28] *The Historical Novel*, p. 122.
[29] *Ibid.*, p. 147.
[30] *Az esztétikum sajátossága*, II, p. 473.

in common with the normal conflicts of everyday life."[31] Lukács has said that the immediacy of the aesthetic effect is a characteristic in all arts; however, because of its public character it is of special importance in drama. The public character of drama demands that all actions and characters be immediately intelligible. The action must move forward with each part of the dialogue, which is possible only if each statement fulfills several functions at the same time. Highly condensed meaning, high degree of clarity, consequently relative simplicity, are further characteristics of the drama, yet, at the same time, each play "must represent a new and peculiar quality," so that "it can exercise the broad and deep impact upon . . . the multitude."[32] These "public" characteristics, plus the fact that man in the drama (more than in the epic), especially man as social-moral being, is emphatically the center of things, make drama much more spiritual than the epic.

Lukács finds that it is difficult to portray life publicly in modern drama because modern life is private. Greek life was public, hence the open, public character of Greek dramas, in which the chorus was a natural factor taken from life itself. Modern dramatists (Shakespeare, Pushkin, Schiller, Goethe) have tried to solve this problem through the use of crowd scenes. However, while in Greek drama the chorus was "omnipresent," the crowd scenes in modern drama are "isolated factors." One modern drama considered by Lukács to be a good example of the blending of public and private lives is Büchner's *Danton's Death*, in which the "scenes follow one another as it were in question-and-answer form, the question raised in one scene being answered in the next, and so on."[33]

[31] *The Historical Novel*, p. 129.
[32] *Ibid.*   [33] *Ibid.*, p. 135.

Seemingly, it would follow from Lukács' demand for drama with "public character" that he would consider the most public sides of modern life (e.g., politics) to be the best material for drama. However, that would be inconsistent with his concept of totality. Concentrating on politics, for example, would result in abstraction, giving the impression of an autonomy of political life. If drama is to reflect the "totality of movement," its center should be the conflict arising out of "human passions," which give expression to all of the bases (social, political, ethical, etc.) of a situation of life.

Finally, Lukács comments briefly on the relationship of the drama and the theatre. While drama has an "autonomous aesthetic existence," he does not believe that theatre, as an art, can exist independently of drama. Again, as so often, he points to the Greek and Elizabethan theatres to show that great theatre coincides with great drama. Both are essential, of course, for, while only playwrights can create the great dramatic types, only the actors can perform it for the public. Lukács sees the "immortality" of the art of acting in that great actors perform "differently in different ages"—the great dramatic characters, for example Hamlet and Falstaff—and thus become "important links" in the chain of such interpretations. In relation to this, he argues that the case is different with film-acting, where "the actor's performance becomes final"; it is not an interpretation of a type already existing in literature, but "an independent creation" of a type, an important part of which is the "actor's personality."[34] Of course, the art of film is different in its entirety from the art of the theatre. While the film portrays every element, every detail (background, actor,

[34] *Az esztétikum sajátossága*, II, p. 474.

etc.), as qualitatively equal parts of its "reality," in the theatre a "hierarchically split" reality comes into being, because the reality of the actor is experienced qualitatively differently than the reality of sets, properties, and costumes.[35] The actor is by far the most important single element in the theatre. Lukács opposes the "dualism" of the man (actor) and background in the theatre, the intrusion of the visual reinforcement (external to the actor), which can only inadequately "copy" or "arbitrarily destroy or falsify" what has already been perfectly expressed in the words.[36] He rejects both the "milieu-stage" (naturalism) and the "mood-stage" (impressionism, turn-of-the-century symbolism) in favor of the Shakespearean, Brechtian theatres, which emphasize the presence of the actor, the man on the stage.[37] This conception of the theatre is wholly consistent with his theory of the drama, which features character and conflict as its central moving force.

[35] Ibid., p. 478.
[36] György Lukács, Világirodalom, 1 (Budapest, 1970), p. 16.
[37] Ibid., p. 17.

10.

THE SOCIAL MISSION
OF ART

It is appropriate once more to return to Lukács'
metaphor describing the relationship between life and
art.[1] In this metaphor art and other "receptive and reproductive forms of a higher order" are compared to some
very unique "tributaries" of the "great river" of life, "tributaries" that originate, branch off from this "river," and
feed back into it only to repeat the entire process again
and again, endlessly. This is a carefully constructed metaphor, consistent with Lukács' materialistic philosophy,
for the "tributary" of art does not originate from mystical
realms but rather from objective reality, the needs of
social life, reflecting these in accordance with the principles peculiar to aesthetics. It is consistent also with
Lukács' belief in art's positive role in improving the
"quality of life" by contributing to the aesthetic-ethical
growth of the "total man." The "tributary" of art does
not bring new "waters" from unknown sources to enlarge
the "river"; it returns the old "waters" in a purified, qualitatively improved form. The qualitative changes result
from the artists' observation of the aesthetic principles
of realistic reflection, type, totality, artistic language, and
the relationship of form and content, as he treats the
materials ("waters") of life. The success of the aesthetic

[1] György Lukács, *Az esztétikum sajátossága*, I (Budapest,
1969), pp. 9-10.

effect (the "feeding back" of the "tributary" into the "river of life") depends entirely upon the successful application of these principles. The "tributary" does not flow back into life in general, but directly into the veins of individual, concrete men during the catharsis, thus storing, accumulating, the potential means for the improvement of society, of life. Since art does not address itself to specific, practical social problems and issues, it promotes the solution of those only indirectly, through the contributions of the ethically-aesthetically improved man.

Consistently with this view of the role of art in society, Lukács rejects (as we have seen) the Stalinist "engineers of the soul" theory, which would make useful tools of art and artists in the accomplishment of timely social tasks. The literature, for example, arising out of such theoretical bases, does not start with the concrete man with his own inner contradictions; rather, it "decorates" its characters with the relatively abstract traits of the framework of a large, current social conflict: "Montage-like, they placed men as positive and negative forces into this framework and tailored their characteristics to fit the given practical tasks. Naturally, they frequently felt that the oversimplifications of this black-white method were so great that it could not deeply move the readers; thus, such scholastic questions emerged as whether and to what degree may a positive hero have negative characteristics (may he at times be, for example, absentminded or lose his temper)."[2] Thus, Lukács rejects the position that art should be propaganda through didactic and rhetorical means. With equal stress, he also rejects the other extreme position that art is for itself, that it has

2 *Az esztétikum sajátossága*, ii, p. 806.

nothing to do with what is happening in society, that it is independent of society, history, ethics, and thought, that there are no guides for aesthetic content and form.[3] Such an extreme conception would have art primarily to give pleasure by creating illusion, dreams, and psychological "intoxication," shoving aside objective reality as less real, less beautiful, and less important than the "transcendence" perceived and experienced through "art." Such "art," like the other extreme, has merely a utilitarian value, because, similarly to drugs and alcohol, it is a commodity designed to make its recipients temporarily feel better by lifting them out of reality, allowing them to forget their problems, to lose their consciousness. Contrary to this, true art makes it possible for man to gain a broader and deeper consciousness of his development, putting the perspective of his life into a clearer focus so that he knows where he comes from and what direction he is going, and creating in him a "moral readiness" to participate positively in society and life.

A more concrete exploration of the social mission of art leads Lukács to the examination of the existing conditions in capitalist and socialist societies. The single most important factor in this regard, he believes, is the relationship between the artist and society. While capitalist societies take pride in allowing the greatest amount of freedom for artistic creation, Lukács asserts that this freedom is really an illusion. There is not a social mission of operation here; it is not an "understood" fact that the society has "entrusted" its artists to create as ancient societies had done.[4] In capitalist societies the artist is a producer of a merchandise; therefore, though seemingly

[3] György Lukács, *Magyar irodalom—magyar kultúra* (Budapest, 1970), p. 385.
[4] *Az esztétikum sajátossága*, I, p. 397.

his freedom is great, he is in fact ruled by the laws of the marketplace, his attitude toward his work is dependent upon the hidden laws of the society. The artist has "subjective freedom" to portray what he wants and how he wants it, but the objective laws of the market push him increasingly in the direction of "individuality" and "individual mannerisms," causing him to "turn inside." The direct relationship between the individual and society has loosened considerably during the past two centuries. The artist's social mission is only unclearly realized through indirect, circuitous avenues. As a result, the artist becomes submerged in self-examination: "first artistic being, then art itself appears problematic, and from this situation more and more self-tormenting and pessimistic thoughts are born about human nature and the human values of the artistic attitude."[5] In capitalist societies "for the sake of subjective freedom, modern art has given up the effort to conquer the objective world."[6] The modern artist has given up the real freedom of art: that the totality of man's world finds its deepest and broadest expression in him. Lukács quotes Ortega y Gasset's statement that "the poet is born where the man ceases to be man,"[7] as an unfortunately accurate summary of the problem of modern bourgeois art.

Further amplifying the problem is the capitalist division of labor. The constant development of the forces of production makes it possible for people, on the one hand, to develop new abilities, but, on the other hand, it makes out of them slaves of their specialties. Advanced capitalist societies have also provided man with more "free time," which, both Marx and Lukács believe, is

[5] Ibid.
[6] Magyar irodalom—magyar kultúra, p. 396.
[7] Ibid., p. 400.

145

"the material basis of every culture."[8] Lukács' concept of "free time," however, includes the existence of favorable mental, psychological, and physical conditions for life as essential factors that capitalism has not been able to provide. While modern philosophers like Nietzsche, in seeking a solution to this problem, look nostalgically into the past, considering slave society most ideal for cultural development, Lukács looks to the future, to the achievement of "free time" with ideal living conditions in advanced, socialist societies.

In socialism there is no artistic freedom in the sense of capitalism's "subjective freedom" for the artist. "Guided" art in socialism means to bring art into direct relationship with the people, the working class, as ancient art was in direct relationship with the "citoyen." Lukács admits that in presently existing socialist societies the social conditions necessary for this are only in the making. The concept of "guidance" is not meant to be realized in the form of bureaucratic control and prescription; rather, it is meant to be "self-guidance," although not independently of the development of society.[9] Great art, he asserts, has always been created by such "self-guidance," resulting in the inseparable unity of realism and humanism, portraying man's totality and guarding man's integrity.[10]

Socialism, he believes, will eliminate the adverse effects of the division of labor by removing the artificial, abstractly existing contradiction between work and pleasure. Art's social mission is to help create and to guard the integrity of the "total man" in both art and life. In

[8] *Ibid.*, p. 311.   [9] *Ibid.*, p. 405.
[10] György Lukács, *Marx és Engels irodalomelmélete* (Budapest, 1949), p. 160.

146

fact, the often rigid distinction between life and art will also disappear, because the "total man" is a kind of "renaissance man." "Man's totality" means the full realization that there is no aspect of human, individual life which is not also a part of community life.[11] The objective, which art will assist in achieving, is the development of an all-sided, "total" social-human personality. Lukács' most influential teacher, Marx, expresses essentially the same thoughts simply and clearly: "With a communist organization of society, the artist is not confined by the local and national seclusion which ensues solely from the division of labor, nor is the individual confined to one specific art, so that he becomes exclusively a painter, a sculptor, etc.; these very names express sufficiently the narrowness of his professional development and his dependence on the division of labor. In a communist society, there are no painters, but at most men who, among other things, also paint."[12] Lukács would deny that this is utopianism. He is not discouraged by the fact that overpopulation and rapidly advancing technology are further magnifying rather than alleviating the problem of the division of labor today, not only in capitalist but also in socialist countries. The ontological views held by him reveal the conviction that there is no preconceived grand plan for man's, for society's, development, nor an end to the development; there is only a direction that is alterable and altered by men depending upon the degree of their awareness, including self-awareness. The "alterable" direction is communism, with science and art providing the means for the necessary expansion of man's

[11] *Magyar irodalom—magyar kultúra*, p. 318.
[12] Mikhail Lifshitz, *The Philosophy of Art of Karl Marx* (New York, 1938), pp. 92-93.

awareness and self-awareness. The achievement of the goal, therefore, depends entirely on men. Since Lukács' humanism invests great faith in men, a faith he verifies from his reading of history, perhaps his Marxist view of the future of art and society is best described as optimistic rather than utopian.

LIST OF WORKS CONSULTED

1. WORKS BY LUKÁCS IN HUNGARIAN

Lukács, György. *Adalékok az esztétika történetéhez* (Contributions to the History of Aesthetics). Budapest: Akadémiai Kiadó, 1953.

——. *Balzac, Stendhal, Zola.* Budapest: Hungária Nyomda Rt., 1945.

——. *A dráma formája* (The Form of the Drama). Budapest, 1909. Offprint from the *Budapesti Szemle.*

——. *Esztétikai kultúra.* (Aesthetic Culture) Budapest: Athenaeum, 1913.

——. "Az esztétikai visszatükrözés problémája" ("The Problem of Aesthetic Reflection"). From the publications of the Hungarian Academy of Sciences, VI, Nos. 2-4, 1955.

——. *Az esztétikum sajátossága* (The Peculiarity of Aesthetics), translated from the German by István Eörsi. 2 vols. Budapest: Akadémiai Kiadó, 1969. Its original German title is *Die Eigenart das Ästhetischen.* Berlin: Luchterhand, 1963.

——. *Az ész trónfosztása* (The Dethronement of Reason). Third edition. Budapest: Akadémiai Kiadó, 1965. German edition: *Die Zerstörung der Vernunft.* Berlin: Aufbau, 1954.

——. "A haladás és reakció harca a mai kultúrában" (The Battle of Progressive and Reactionary Forces in Today's Culture). Budapest: Szikra, 1956. An address given before the Political Academy of the Hungarian Workers' Party on June 28, 1956.

149

Lukács, György. *Írástudók felelossége* (The Responsibility of Intellectuals). Budapest: Szikra Kiadás. 1945.

———. "Az irodalomtörténet reviziója és az irodalom-tanitás" (The Revision of the History of Literature and the Teaching of Literature). Budapest, 1948. An address delivered before the meeting of the Hungarian Teachers' Union on October 28, 1948.

———. *A kapitalista kultúra csődje* (The Bankruptcy of Capitalist Culture). Budapest: Szikra, 1949.

———. "A különös esztétikai problémája a felvilágosodásban és Goethénél" (The Problem of Specialty in Aesthetics in the Enlightenment and with Goethe). Offprint from the *Magyar Tudomány*, Nos. 4-6, 1956.

———. *A különösség, mint esztétikai kategória* (Specialty, as a Category of Aesthetics). Budapest: Akadémiai Kiadó, 1957. Title of German edition: *Über die Besonderheit als Kategorie der Aesthetik.* Neuwied: Luchterhand, 1967.

———. *Lenin.* Budapest: Magvető, 1970. Original German edition: *Lenin.* Berlin: Malik Verlag, 1924.

———. *Magyar irodalom—magyar kultúra* (Hungarian Literature—Hungarian Culture). Budapest: Gondolat Kiadó, 1970. A collection of essays, articles, reviews, and interviews published between 1903 and 1969.

———. *Marx és Engels irodalomelmélete* (The Literary Theories of Marx and Engels). Budapest: Szikra Kiadás, 1949. German edition: *Karl Marx und Friedrich Engels als Literaturhistoriker.* Berlin: Aufbau, 1948.

———. *A marxi esztétika alapjai* (The Bases of Marxist Aesthetics). Budapest: Szikra Kiadás, 1947.

———. "Megjegyzések az irodalomtörténet elméletéhez"

(Notes on the Theory of Literary History). Offprint from the *Alexander-Emlékkönyv*, 1910.

———. *Művészet és társadalom* (Art and Society). Budapest: Gondolat Kiadó, 1968. Contains selected studies in aesthetics originally published in German and Hungarian.

———. "A művészet mint felépitmény" (Art as Superstructure). A special publication of the Hungarian Cultural Ministry, 1955.

———. *Nagy orosz realisták* (Great Russian Realists). Budapest: Szikra Kiadás, 1946.

———. *Nagy orosz realisták, kritikai realizmus* (Great Russian Realists, Critical Realism). Budapest: Szikra, 1951. Contains some of the essays published in the 1946 edition.

———. "Népi irók a mérlegen" (Folk-writers on the Scale). Budapest: Szikra Kiadás, 1946. An address given before the Political Academy of the Hungarian Communist Party on March 2, 1946.

———. *A polgári filozófia válsága* (The Crisis of Bourgeois Philosophy). Budapest: Hungária, 1947.

———. *A realizmus problémái* (The Problems of Realism), translated from the German by Endre Gáspár. Budapest: Athenaeum, 1948. German edition: *Essays über Realismus*. Berlin: Aufbau, 1948.

———. "Sztálin cikkeinek tanúlságai az irodalom és művészettörténet szempontjából" (The Lessons of Stalin's articles from the Point of View of the History of Literature and Art). Offprint from the publications of the Hungarian Academy of Sciences, I, No. 1.

———. *Az újabb német irodalom rövid története* (A Short History of Recent German Literature). Budapest: Athenaeum, 1946. German edition: *Skizze*

einer Geschichte der neueren deutschen Literatur.
Berlin: Aufbau, 1953.

Lukács, György. *Új magyar kultúráét* (Toward a New
Hungarian Culture). Budapest: Szikra Kiadás, 1948.

————. *Utam Marxhoz* (My Road to Marx). 2 vols.
Budapest: Magvetö Könyvkiadó, 1971. Contains
selected essays on politics, philosophy, and
aesthetics.

————. *Világirodalom* (World Literature). 2 vols. Budapest: Gondolat Kiadó, 1970.

2. WORKS BY LUKÁCS IN ENGLISH

Lukács, Georg. *Essays on Thomas Mann,* trans. Stanley
Mitchell. New York: Grosset & Dunlap, 1965.

————. *Goethe and His Age,* trans. Robert Anchor. New
York: Grosset & Dunlap, 1969.

————. *The Historical Novel,* trans. Hannah and Stanley Mitchell. London: Merlin Press, 1962.

————. *History and Class Consciousness: Studies in
Marxist Dialectics,* trans. Rodney Livingstone. Cambridge: MIT Press, 1971.

————. *Realism in Our Time,* trans. John and Necke
Mander; Introduction by George Steiner. New
York: Harper and Row, Publishers, 1964. The text
is the same as that of *The Meaning of Contemporary Realism.*

————. *Studies in European Realism,* introd. by Alfred
Kazin. New York: Grosset & Dunlap, 1964.

————. *The Theory of the Novel,* trans. Anna Bostock.
Cambridge: MIT Press, 1971.

————. *Writer and Critic,* trans. Arthur Kahn. London:
Merlin Press, 1970. Contains a group of essays
selected by the translator.

3. BOOKS IN ENGLISH WHOLLY OR PARTLY ABOUT LUKÁCS

Aczél, T., and Méray, T. *The Revolt of the Mind.* New York: Praeger, 1959.

Arvon, Henri. *Marxist Esthetics,* translated from the French by Helen R. Lane. Ithaca: Cornell University Press, 1973.

Bahr, Ehrhard and Kunzer, Ruth G. *Georg Lukács.* New York: Frederick Ungar Publishing Co., 1972.

Demetz, Peter. *Marx, Engels and the Poets.* Chicago: The University of Chicago Press, 1967.

Jameson, Fredric. *Marxism and Form.* Princeton: Princeton University Press, 1971.

Labedz, Leopold, ed. *Revisionism: Essays on the History of Marxist Ideas.* New York: Frederick A. Praeger, 1962.

Lichtheim, George. *George Lukács.* New York: The Viking Press, 1970.

Mészáros, István. *Aspects of History and Class Consciousness.* London: Routledge, 1971.

Parkinson, G.H.R., ed. *Georg Lukács, The Man, His Work and His Ideas.* New York: Vintage Books, 1970.

Sontag, Susan. *Against Interpretation.* New York: Dell Publishing Co., Inc., 1969.

Tőkés, Rudolf L. *Béla Kun and the Hungarian Soviet Republic.* New York: Frederick A. Praeger, for the Hoover Institution, Stanford University, 1967.

Váli, F. A. *Rift and Revolt in Hungary.* Cambridge, Mass.: Harvard U. Press and London: Oxford U. Press, 1961.

Zitta, Victor. *Georg Lukács' Marxism: Alienation, Dialectics, Revolution: A Study in Utopia and Ideology.* The Hague: Martinus Nijhoff, 1961.

4. ARTICLES ABOUT LUKÁCS IN ENGLISH
   LANGUAGE PERIODICALS

Demetz, Peter. "The Uses of Lukács." *Yale Review*, LIV (1965), 435-40.

Deutscher, Isaac. "Georg Lukács and 'Critical Realism.'" *The Listener*, November 3, 1966, 659-62.

Elvin, H. L. "Marx and the Marxists as Literary Critics." *Journal of Adult Education*, X (1938), 260-76.

Glicksberg, Charles I. "The Aberrations of Marxist Criticism." *Queens Quarterly*, LVI (1949), 479-90.

———. "Literature and the Marxist Aesthetic." *University of Toronto Quarterly*, XVIII (1949), 76-84.

Heller, Ágnes. "Lukács' Aesthetics." *The New Hungarian Quarterly*, VII (1966), No. 24, 84-94.

Hyman, Stanley Edgar. "The Marxist Criticism of Literature." *Antioch Review*, VII (1947), 541-68.

Kettle, A. Review of *Studies in European Realism. The Modern Quarterly*, VI/1 (Winter 1950-1951), 72-81.

Lichtheim, George. "An Intellectual Disaster." *Encounter*, XX (May 1963), 74-80.

Maslow, Vera. "Georg Lukács and the Unconscious." *The Journal of Aesthetics and Art Criticism*, XXII (1964), 465-70.

———. "Lukács' man-centered aesthetics." *Philosophy and Phenomenological Research*, XXVII (1967), 242-52.

Mitchell, Stanley. "Georg Lukács and the Historical Novel." *Marxism Today*, December 1963, 374-82.

Rieser, M. "Lukács' Critique of German Philosophy." *The Journal of Philosophy*, LV (1958), 177-96.

Steiner, George. "Georg Lukács and his Devil's Pact." *The Kenyon Review*, Winter 1960, 1-18.

Watnick, Morris. "Georg Lukács: An Intellectual Biography." *Soviet Survey*, No. 23 (1958), 60-66; No. 24 (1958), 51-57; No. 25 (1958), 61-68; No. 27 (1959), 75-81.

5. RELATED WORKS AND REFERENCES

Childe, V. Gordon. *Man Makes Himself.* London: Watts & Co., 1936.

Filozófiai Lexikon. Budapest: Szikra, 1953.

Hegel, G.W.F. *The Phenomenology of the Mind,* trans. J. B. Baillie. New York: Humanities Press, Inc., 1966.

————. *The Philosophy of Fine Art,* trans. F.P.B. Osmaston, Vol. I. London: G. Bell and Sons, Ltd., 1920.

Kierkegaard, S. *Fear and Trembling,* trans. Walter Lowrie. Princeton: Princeton University Press, 1941.

Lessing, G. E. *Hamburg Dramaturgy,* trans. Helen Zimmern. New York: Dover Publication, Inc., 1962.

Lifshitz, Mikhail. *The Philosophy of Art of Karl Marx.* New York: Critics Group, 1938.

Mehring, Franz. *Die Lessing-Legende.* Berlin: Dietz Verlag, 1963.

INDEX

acting, 50, 140
action, 59-60, 65, 90, 99, 105, 126; dramatic, 129, 131f, 139
Adorno, Theodor W., 14; *Noten zur Literatur*, 14
Ady, Endre, 6-7
Aeschylus, 59, 62, 101, 112; *The Oresteia*, 137; *The Persians*, 117; *Prometheus Bound*, 137
aesthetic effect, 16, 50, 53, 61, 79, 106, 110, 113-124f, 139, 142f
aesthetic form, *see* form
aesthetic laws, 76
aesthetics, bourgeois, 137
alienation, 9, 24, 49, 63, 84f, 100; effect, 95
allegorical style, 51
allegory, 14, 16, 74f, 95-102
Antoine, Andre, 5
Aristophanes, 117
Aristotle, 15f, 21, 26, 37, 50, 54f, 59, 66, 71, 73f, 122; *Poetics*, 35, 44, 60
art, value of, 113
art for art's sake, 18, 62, 121
artist and society, 144
artistic sensitivity, 94
avant-gardism, 55
avant-gardist art, 50

Balázs, Béla, 6f

Balzac, Honoré de, 62, 68, 76, 83
Baudelaire, Charles Pierre, 5
beauty, 45, 104: artistic, 116, 122f; natural, 122f
Beckett, Samuel, 64, 66, 100, 114
Benjamin, Walter, 13
Bergson, Henri, 30f, 60, 89
Berkeley, George, 21, 25
Blum theses, 9
bourgeois art, 145
bourgeois literature, 124
Brecht, Bertolt, 95, 117, 121; *Galileo*, 130
Brieux, Eugène, 117
Büchner, Georg, *Danton's Death*, 129, 139

capitalist society, 24; art in, 84, 144-46
catharsis, 61, 116ff, 121, 143
Caudwell, Christopher, 13; *Illusion and Reality*, 13
Cervantes Saavedra, Miguel de, 59, 66
Chamberlain, Houston Stewart, 17
character, 68, 80, 86, 105; dramatic, 111, 130f, 135, 139ff; tragic, 119; typical, 106, 112; typical-symbolic, 130
characterization, 86; dramatic, 66, 107, 131ff, 138

PRINCETON ESSAYS IN LITERATURE

Library of Congress Cataloging in Publication Data

Királyfalvi, Béla, 1937-
   The aesthetics of György Lukács.

   (Princeton essays in literature)
   1. Lukács, György, 1885-1971.   I.   Title.
BH221.H84L865   111.8'5   74-22401
ISBN 0-691-07205-1